Literate Beginnings

Programs for babies and toddlers

Debby Ann Jeffery

American Library Association
Chicago and London
1995

Cover by Tessing Design

Text design and composition by Publishing Services, Inc. in ITC Kabel and
ITC Berkeley on Xyvision/Linotype

Printed on 50-pound Publishers Smooth, a pH-neutral stock, and bound in
10-point C1S cover stock by McNaughton & Gunn, Inc.

The paper used in this publication meets the minimum requirements of
American National Standard for Information Sciences—Permanence of Paper
for Printed Library Materials, ANSI Z39.48-1992. ∞

Library of Congress Cataloging-in-Publication Data
Jeffery, Debby Ann.
    Literate beginnings : programs for babies and toddlers / by Debby Ann
Jeffery.
        p.   cm.
    Includes bibliographical references (p.   ) and index.
    ISBN 0-8389-0640-0
    1. Children's libraries—Activity programs—United States.   2. Public
libraries—United States—Services to infants.   3. Public libraries—United
States—Services to toddlers.   I. Title.
Z718.2.U6J44   1995
027.62'5—dc20   95-10691

Printed in the United States of America.

99   98   97   96   5   4   3   2

To my husband Mark

Contents

Preface

Learning begins at birth. Librarians have traditionally provided story times for three- to five-year-olds and more recently for toddlers, but it is important to introduce children to books and libraries at an even earlier age. Young children's intellectual development is faster than that of any other age group. "Babies need books," to quote Dorothy Butler, and they also need baby-toddler times. San Francisco Public Library, where I work, has been offering these popular, easy-to-master programs, called "Lapsits" since 1981.

This book is for people who are considering programming for babies and toddlers. Both the beginning librarian and the seasoned professional will find many helpful programs and programming ideas. Libraries that now offer toddler times can easily alter their programs to incorporate babies by adding more finger games and songs and using fewer books. Many toddler times already have babies tagging along with older brother or sister, and here is a way to involve them in the program. I have provided recommendations for planning and presentation along with an annotated bibliography of programming books and audiovisual materials, as well as helpful tips for getting started and quickly producing a program. Part 2, "Program Activity Sheets," contains fifty-two ready-to-use programs which can be used as is or changed in any way for a more personalized program. Each program comes with an instruction sheet and suggested books.

The benefits to children of this type of programming are numerous. Caregivers and librarians alike report positive results, including increased comprehension and attention spans and early language acquisition. Perhaps what is most important is that children want to come to the library and enjoy getting together as a group. They demand to be read to and appreciate books. The goal of the program is not to create "super" babies who read by the age of three, but to set the stage for lifelong readers who will in turn share books and finger games with their young children. The process of learning to read can be trying for anyone. The school child who already loves books and literature will be more motivated to learn this essential skill.

The entire family profits from baby-toddler programs. Baby-toddler programs remind caregivers that it is important to talk, sing, and read with their children.

Programs give suggestions for appropriate materials and demonstrate how to share them. Caregivers will learn about nursery rhymes, finger games, recorded music, and the many wonderful picture stories to share with their children. In effect, programs are literary parenting classes.

Programs also help build a sense of community, creating a forum where information is shared about neighborhood activities and friendships are fostered. The group at the Potrero branch of the San Francisco Public Library formed a baby-sitting cooperative. Other branches report program participants forming regular potluck dinners and play groups.

Your library will also benefit from baby-toddler programming in wonderful and sometimes unexpected ways. In San Francisco, picture book circulation rose at some locations as much as 30 percent. Baby-toddler program audiences were the most vocal and active when budget cuts and library closures threatened. These programs attract attention from the news media as well. San Francisco Public Library has received local and national television and newspaper coverage. Everyone loves babies and books.

The activity sheets in this book have evolved over an eleven-year period of baby-toddler programming. During this time I have trained other librarians, participated in several workshops, sent out written materials to professionals all over the country, and spoken to many about this program. I have gathered material from numerous sources, including librarians who shared their program ideas with me. I have also created and adapted to suit a particular theme. I have not been a writer so much as a borrower and compiler.

Please feel free to use the activity sheets in any way you want and most important, have fun with them. Many librarians report this is their favorite program once they get their feet wet. Come on in; the water's fine!

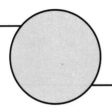

Acknowledgments

I wish to thank Neel Parikh for suggesting that I write the *School Library Journal* article and for her support of the program while she was at San Francisco Public Library. I want to acknowledge Grace Ruth for her valuable assistance with collection development for this work and for all our children's collections. My gratitude to Helen Cannon, Joyce Dixon, Susan Faust, and especially Ellen Mahoney for developing the original programs. Without Ellen Mahoney's encouragement, this book never would have been written. I also wish to thank Judith Faria, Linda Geistlinger, Joan Goldman, Mark Hall, Anna Holmboe, Carla Kozak, Irene Lee, John Philbrook, Shelley Sorenson, Donna Trifilo, Karey Wehner, Audrey Wood, and the other "Lapsitting" librarians who have shared their ideas and materials with me and have kept the program alive and well. Special thanks to my niece, Sue Moenter, for her assistance in editing; my first editor at ALA Editions, Bonnie Smothers, who could envision this book from the beginning; and my second editor, Patrick Hogan, for his help in finishing this project.

Permissions

Here are Grandma's spectacles, Clap your hands, Cobbler, cobbler, mend my shoe, Leg over leg, Hickory dickory dock, This little piggy went to market, This is my father, This is my garden, Way up high in the apple tree, Pat-a-cake, pat-a-cake, from *Let's Do Fingerplays* by Marion Grayson, 1962. Available from Robert B. Luce, c/o Integrated Distribution, 195 McGregor St., Manchester, NH 03102.

This is the way the ladies ride, Here's a ball for baby, Round and round the cornfield, This little piggy went to market, Shoe a little horse, Pussy cat, pussy cat, Baa baa black sheep, Old mother goose, Hey diddle diddle, To market, to market, One I love, from *Lavender's Blue* by Kathleen Lines (1954). Used by permission of Oxford University Press

Paws, muzzles, ears and tails, ears and tails and Do you know the muffin man/Now we have the latke man reprinted with permission of Carla Kozak

MY DREYDL, Music by S. E. Goldfarb; Arranged by H. C.; Words by S. S. Grossman, from *The Songs We Sing,* selected and edited by Harry Coopersmith. Copyright 1950 by The United Synagogue of America. Utilized with permission of the publisher, The United Synagogue Commission on Jewish Education

Clap your hands, Eentsy weentsy spider, Five happy valentines, Five little babies, Fun with hands, Halloween is here, If you're happy and you know it, I'm bouncing, Little leaves, Open, shut them, Quacking ducks, Row, row, row your boat, Teapot, The stars, The sun, Ten little fingers, What am I, Wheels on the bus, from *Ring A Ring O' Roses,* 1971. Published courtesy of Flint Public Library, Flint, Michigan

"Boing Boing Squeak" from THE NEW KID ON THE BLOCK by Jack Prelutsky. Copyright © 1984 by Jack Prelutsky. Used with permission of Greenwillow Books, a division of William Morrow & Company, Inc., and Reed Consumer Books, Ltd., England

Eye winker, tom tinker from *Eye Winker, Tom Tinker, Chin Chopper* by Tom Glazer (Doubleday, 1973). Reprinted with permission

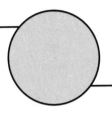

Introduction

Baby-toddler programs may be the most important service your library offers. What can be more important than helping caregivers and their very young children explore and conquer the world of literature? This book has been written to assist librarians and other interested adults in beginning baby-toddler programs using a variety of literature, from songs and books to finger games. I have attempted to compile the best books and other materials available for very young children and show how to present them to a group of caregivers and their children, from birth to age five. The book has been divided into two distinct sections: the chapters and the activity sheets. Try to avoid going straight to Part 2, as the introductory chapters have many suggestions for getting the most out of the program activity sheets.

Each chapter covers elements important to successful programming. The benefits of baby-toddler programs are explored, including early childhood development and the importance of literature and language in the process. Planning, presentation, and evaluation are covered to give professionals many suggestions and ideas for beginning this type of program as well as tips for success. The importance of picture stories as a programming element is covered, as are suggested criteria for the evaluation of good read-alouds. Oral folklore traditions play a major role in baby-toddler programs. Nursery rhymes, finger games, and songs are introduced along with ways of using them for maximum benefit. Last comes the chapter on the use of multimedia materials including musical instruments, puppets, felt boards, simple crafts, recorded music, and video.

Part 2 contains fifty-two program sheets, accompanying instructions, and book recommendations. Readers may use them as is, make a few changes, or use the ideas as the basis for creating their own programs. Most of them are theme related because I enjoy programming that way, but many librarians never use themes. Themes are not necessary for successful programs.

The annotated bibliography of picture books, all sure winners for baby-toddler times, will help professionals quickly identify books to use in programs. Picture books develop listening and looking skills and are an important element of the program. They expand a child's world and motivate that child to read when the time comes. There is a suggested list of further reading and resources, listing song books and collections of poems and nursery rhymes, which will help librarians find sources for more material. This list of titles for further reading includes the classic *Babies Need Books,* which is highly recommended for understanding the importance of introducing very young children to literature.

I hope this book will be a guide and an inspiration for other librarians and libraries to connect very young children with their literary heritage.

PART 1

Successful Baby-Toddler Programming

CHAPTER 1

Baby-Toddler Programs and Child Development

Baby-toddler programs are designed to serve two different populations: the caregiver and the child. Each has separate literary, informational, and social needs that can be met by the programs presented in this book. A single well-designed program can introduce literature and libraries to both the caregiver and child.

○ THE CAREGIVER

The term caregiver has emerged because many children are not being raised by traditional "parents." In this book, caregiver means parent, grandparent, nanny, baby-sitter or any other person who brings the child to the baby-toddler program.

Much has been written about the merits of reading to young children, but many new caregivers may need help selecting and sharing appropriate materials from the vast array available. This information is available at baby-toddler programs. Caregivers learn what kind of books to choose, as well as how to read them in an engaging manner. By watching the librarian demonstrate finger games, they are reminded of rhymes and songs from their past or they learn new ones. All this information, in the form of books and handouts, goes home to reinforce this newly acquired knowledge. These programs are literary parenting classes.

Baby-toddler programs also play an important social role. Young families meet and exchange information, form play groups, and develop friendships with people with other young children. This is particularly important in a mobile society. It is not unusual at all for family and friends to be scattered all over the country or the world, leaving adults with young children isolated, without the age-old supports of extended families, etc. After the Lapsit at the Mercer branch in San Francisco, most of the audience would reconvene at the park down the street.* At the Potrero branch program in San Francisco, parents formed a baby-sitting co-op, a play group, and scheduled a monthly potluck dinner at the local community center.

The caregivers who attend this program often report that it provides quality time for them to be with their child. It makes them feel good because they know they are doing something beneficial for both. Adults also reported that they just plain enjoy coming together with other people to share the joys of books, songs, and finger games.

Caregivers new to this country and the English language come for the reasons mentioned above, but also to improve their own language skills while introducing the child to American culture and literature. I had a young Vietnamese mother and baby come to every program and record it. During the week, she and her baby would practice using the tape and the handout until the next program. The mother and child quickly mastered the program materials and felt comfortable with them.

* These programs are called Infant-Toddler Lapsits at the San Francisco Public Library because the younger attendees spend most of their time in someone's lap.

There are very few places or services that cater to children from birth to three years of age and their caregivers. By providing baby-toddler programs, the library is inviting people with young children to use the library. It says they are welcome, whether they attend every program or not. Caregivers have an opportunity to ask about books on parenting, sources for children's services in the area, and other information. This is the librarian's opportunity to help these young families in using the whole collection and community. It is important to get these young people into the library. They are the future. One day they may be deciding whether a public library is necessary or not. If we can introduce these families to the magic and vistas the library has to offer, both they and the library will benefit.

○ THE CHILD

The child from birth to three years of age goes through some incredible developmental stages, some of the most important in his or her life. According to Dorothy Butler in her book *Babies Need Books,* books can make a dramatic difference in the development of a child. Learning begins at birth. "Scientists tell us that approximately one half of a person's ultimate intelligence is developed by the age of four."[1]

There are many fine books on child development. Try *Your Child: Birth to Age Six* by Fitzhugh Dodson and Ann Alexander[2] for easy-to-access sections on development or the books by Penelope Leach, *Your Baby and Child: From Birth to Age Five*[3] or *Babyhood: Stage by Stage.*[4] In this book, only highlights of child development will be discussed in the context of the influence of baby-toddler programs. Specifically, children who regularly attend a program tend to develop earlier than their peers. Librarians and caregivers alike report accelerated language and motor development and longer reading spans. This means that the one-year-old will be enjoying books normally thought of for a two-year-old, the two-year-old will appreciate books generally used with a three-year-old, and so on. Book selection is often one to two years above that of other children who regularly visit the library. Librarians who offer baby-toddler programs are not advocating creating "super" babies,

or teaching them math with flash cards. The goal is to develop a lifelong reader and lover of books and libraries.

Birth to Age One

Caregivers of newborns quickly learn there is magic in the sound of their voice. They can calm the baby with just a few words or put her or him to sleep with a song. A newborn can distinguish his or her primary caregiver's voice from all other voices within two or three days following birth. A baby draws security from knowing this person is near and one of the strongest reassurances is the voice. But, what to say and how to say it?

During a baby-toddler program the librarian acts as a catalyst, introducing material and showing how to use it. For many adults, participating in the program is easy as they remember songs and rhymes from their childhood. The baby will not understand the words but will respond to the sounds of lyrical and rhythmical poetry and song. It is easy to incorporate materials for the newborn into the baby-toddler program. Lullabies and simple nursery rhymes appeal to a wide age range. Two excellent collections are *The Lullaby Songbook* by Jane Yolen and *Trot Trot to Boston: Play Rhymes for Baby* by Carol F. Ra.[5] Foot and hand patting works well with young children. When the rhyme "Cobbler, Cobbler" is in the program, caregivers can pat the foot of their very young child while others in the audience can join in by clapping their hands.[6] At this stage the parent is the more active participant.

By six months, if not sooner, visual acuity is established. The baby can now focus on objects farther away. Children of this age will really begin to see the baby-toddler program, watching the librarian and other people and trying to perform finger games. They will enjoy the countless games adults can play with them. Finger games that are tickles, bounces, jiggles, and foot and hand pats should be incorporated into the program. Caregivers can exercise their baby and amuse them for long periods of play. Lap jogs such as "To Market, To Market" (RMG, p. 19) can be favorites of this age group and older children as well.* One of the

---

* Unless otherwise noted, all cited nursery rhymes are from *The Real Mother Goose* (New York: Checkerboard Press, 1916). Page numbers are given in parentheses.

best sources for these simple games is Norah Montgomerie's *This Little Pig Went to Market. The Real Mother Goose,* published by Checkerboard Press, is also a wonderful source. Simple books, such as Helen Oxenbury's *All Fall Down* and *Clap Hands,* can now be appreciated by these children when they are used in a program.

By nine months a few words may begin to emerge. The child now knows his or her name. Caregivers should be encouraged to incorporate their babies' names into the rhymes and songs as often as possible. It is music to the little ones' ears. Baby-toddler programs should always have a name song or rhyme for this very reason. "Charlie over the Water"[7] is an old favorite.

By eleven to twelve months old many children are walking. They can clap hands, wave goodbye, and make a fist. The simplest motions are within their capabilities with a little assistance from their caregiver. The action finger games take on more significance now, as some little ones will practically dance their way through a program. Finger games like "¿Donde Está Mi Familia?"[8], sung to the tune of "Frère Jacques,"[9] will be popular. Books such as *"More, More, More," Said the Baby* by Vera Williams and *Across the Stream* by Mirra Ginsburg offer a rich text and a visual treat. By a child's first birthday, he or she may know between three and ten words. The caregiver may be the only one who understands, but here again, names are crucial and the child will give names to significant others in the family. It is not unusual for a child who regularly attends the program to know and say the librarian's name.

It is the librarian's job to help the caregiver surround the young child with language. The one-year-old has traveled from the initial listening stage at birth to the beginning of speech. The first year is pretty amazing!

Age One to Two

The one-year-old knows more words than he or she can speak. But children this age are beginning to appreciate the power of speech and are more motivated than ever to learn new words. Watch how closely they attend to books in which familiar objects are realistically represented, such as *Whose Shoe* by Margaret Miller. This is the time the labeling books come into play so strongly. A great deal

of pointing and naming takes place with a child this age. Leah Wilcox calls this the "look-say" period in language development.[10] Simple books like *Dressing* by Helen Oxenbury serve a real purpose for a young child. When using one in a program the librarian can point to the socks and ask the audience for the answer. Even though it will be the eager two-year-olds who will answer, the younger children will take it all in.

At eighteen months there is a spurt of linguistic development. Vocabulary can actually range from eighteen to twenty-five words with a comprehension level that is much higher. The child is able to vocalize more sounds and will be more astute in learning names of things. Words have gradually become thought symbols.

This is the age of real interest in books, oftentimes beyond those that simply label objects. Participation books such as *Spots, Feathers and Curly Tales* by Tafuri or the "Spot" books by Eric Hill will allow the toddler to interact with the book. This interaction between the child and the librarian during a program can be very satisfying. Some children will prefer special interest books now. Cars and trucks and other things that go are often favorite subjects, nicely treated in books such as *Freight Train* by Donald Crews or *Bus Stop* by Nancy Helen. ABC and number books, particularly those that provide short, cumulative plots, will hold the toddler's attention. *Teddy Bears from 1 to 10* by Susanna Gretz is a good example. These basic concept books, as well as others by Tana Hoban and Bruce McMillan, play an important part in a toddler's education. Such books enable a child to learn about the world and give it order. Programs built around these themes work very well and are always popular.

Toward the end of a child's second year, he or she will begin to enjoy real story books. These should be stories with very simple plots, perhaps cumulative in nature, such as *Mr. Gumpy's Outing* by John Burningham and *The Chick and the Duckling* by Mirra Ginsburg. This is truly a landmark time and it is such fun to introduce a child to these great selections. Many of the best books for young children are in this group.

Equally as exciting is the toddlers' growing appreciation of rhymes, poetry, and songs. As their vocabulary grows, they begin to grasp just what the lovely sounds mean. Original collections of poetry such as *You Be Good and I'll Be Night* by Eve Merriam along with traditional nursery rhymes will engage the toddler. They enjoy the story lines behind "Baa, Baa, Black Sheep" (RMG, p. 58) or "Mary Had a Little Lamb,"[11] and can sing along during the programs.

Finger games take on new dimensions. Where they first appealed for their musical cadence and rhythms, they now offer moments of real pleasure in which the toddler delights in his or her marvelous new ability to master them. Toddlers can stretch and bend, open and close their hands, etc. They can become teapots and eentsy weentsy spiders, or act out the motions to "Row, Row, Row Your Boat."[12] Body rhymes such as "Ten Fingers"[13] or "Eye Winker"[14] teach the names of body parts and reinforce pride in identity. Toddlers are truly pleased with themselves and their literary accomplishments.

Age Two to Three

The two- to three-year-olds are important participants in the baby-toddler program. Many children's librarians already program for this age. Now children are truly beginning to talk. Their vocabulary extends from fifty to one hundred words. This number will double by age two and a half and then again by age three. Sentences will consist of two to three words at age two and the simplest noun-verb combinations will be used. Sentence complexity will develop at a remarkable rate during this year.

The two-year-old's orientation to the world is strictly egocentric. Reality to these children centers solely on themselves and their personal world. It is not that they are selfish. Rather, their experiences do not take them beyond the immediate environment of which they are the center. In order to involve a child of this age, literature must discuss objects and situations he or she already knows. If a fanciful character is introduced, the story's setting and situation must be in accord with the youngster's experiences of reality. Bears can live in a house in the woods, but that house must be filled with everyday objects such as bowls and spoons, chairs and beds. Once the child has a comfortable feeling about the setting of the story, he or she can move on to enjoy different events or

ideas that may add to the growth of new levels of comprehension. The use of literature can help children move away from egocentricity, where everything centers on themselves, to a gradual acceptance of a broader scope of thinking. Esphyr Slobodkinia's *The Wonderful Feast* and *We Have a Baby* by Cathryn Falwell can help in this process.

Now the child can understand and appreciate books with greater depth and longer text. Books such as *Jamberry* by Bruce Degan, with its snappy verse, or *Benny Bakes a Cake* by Eve Rice, with its wonderful birthday story, will delight the older child. Baby-toddler programs can also address transitions common to children's lives, such as starting school or a new baby in the family, and prepare youngsters by helping them deal with confusing feeling and fears. Special interest books continue to fascinate, and so will programs on going to the zoo or birthdays. Concept books are still popular and number books present greater challenges. Another type of concept book coming to the fore is the color concept book. Programs on colors and counting will excite this group and the many books, such as *One, Two, Three to the Zoo* by Eric Carle will fit nicely with all the finger games and songs available on these subjects. Photographic books by Ann Morris, such as *Bread, Bread, Bread,* expand a child's world by revealing a variety of people and life-styles.

As the child nears his or her third birthday, the time for graduation from baby-toddler programs approaches. These children are masters of the materials used in the programs. They still enjoy the songs and finger games and showing the younger children how things are done, but the books used in the programs are too simple now. They have probably been reading much longer stories at home, one on one, for over a year. When they were two the child and caregiver were asking for *Curious George*[15] and other books normally thought of as preschool books. Now the three-year-old needs even more sophisticated stories. Librarians and caregivers report this acceleration in attention span and book level, which may be one accomplishment of the program. A thorough study of the development of children who attend programs versus those who do not would be welcome. Right now we have common sense and observation to support the benefits of baby-toddler programs.

At this stage of development, when true language play begins to emerge, children become even more enamored of rhymes, songs, and poetry. They love to read nursery rhymes in books and editions of single rhymes are ever popular. *Three Little Kittens* by Paul Galdone lends itself well to a program; the presenter can show the pictures while the rhyme is said or sung. Finger-play rhymes, though not great literature, are more fun than ever with this age group. Manual dexterity is developing rapidly now and trickier and trickier manipulations are possible. There are many fine collections of finger games. For patrons there are the Marc Brown and Tom Glazer books, and for the librarian about the best collection of these ever published was *Ring a Ring o' Roses* by the Flint Public Library.

In three short years, the helpless newborn has developed into an active, inquisitive, and very accomplished young library patron. The rewards of this type of programming for children are innumerable. Librarians who present baby-toddler programs feel they have contributed to the development of a happy and satisfied reader. Librarians enjoy watching the wonderful growth and development of the child, and the baby-toddler program is a wonderful way to do so. Many librarians truly become an important person to the young patrons and their families. Caregivers have often reported the positive role librarians and baby-toddler programs have played in their child's life. Young children conduct their own programs at home using finger games, books, and songs with their dolls and stuffed animals. Sometimes they even accompany themselves on toy guitars. One vacationing toddler recruited all his relatives into participating in a homemade program because he missed coming to the library so much. Children's librarians find themselves helping to lay the very foundation for a love of reading and learning that will stay with their young patrons for a lifetime.

Notes

1. Dorothy Butler, *Babies Need Books* (New York: Atheneum, 1980), 1.
2. Fitzhugh Dodson and Ann Alexander, *Your Child: Birth to Age Six* (New York: Simon & Schuster, 1986).
3. Penelope Leach, *Your Baby and Child: From Birth to Age Five,* new ed., rev. and expanded (New York: Knopf, 1989).
4. ———, *Babyhood: Stage by Stage, from Birth to Age Two* (New York: Knopf, 1983).
5. Unless otherwise noted, all books mentioned in the text are included in the annotated bibliographies in the back of this book.
6. *Ring a Ring o' Roses: Stories, Games and Finger Plays for Pre-School Children* (Flint, Mich.: Flint Public Library, 1971), 52.
7. Tom Glazer, *Eye Winker, Tom Tinker, Chin Chopper: Fifty Musical Fingerplays* (New York: Doubleday, 1973), 18.
8. Cynthia Baird, G. Baird, and M. Mena, *Songs and Rhymes/Rimas y Rondas* (South San Francisco, Calif.: South San Francisco Public Library, Children's Services, 1990), 25.
9. *Singing Bee! A Collection of Favorite Children's Songs* (New York: Lothrop, Lee & Shepard, 1982), 134.
10. Ellen Mahoney and Leah Wilcox, *Ready, Set, Read: Best Books to Prepare Preschoolers* (New York: Scarecrow, 1985), 57.
11. *Singing Bee,* 58.
12. Ibid., 135.
13. Glazer, *Eye Winker,* 72.
14. Ibid., 24.
15. H. A. Rey, *Curious George* (New York: Houghton Mifflin, 1941).

CHAPTER 2

Planning, Presenting, and Evaluating Your Programs

The importance of baby-toddler programs cannot be stressed enough. As discussed in the previous chapter, children need literature and libraries. As the twenty-first century approaches, the child population is expected to increase, making the need for this type of program even greater. Furthermore, these programs are popular and rewarding for libraries that offer them. There are many factors to weigh when considering providing such a program. Are babies and toddlers considered a priority at your library? If so, what are the library's goals for this age group? How many programs is the library currently supporting and are there staff and energy available for another? Is there a convenient time slot and location, and does the community contain an interested and available audience?

The purpose of this chapter is threefold. First, to demonstrate how to plan programs while keeping preparation time to a minimum. Second, to demonstrate implementing a program using the ideas and activity sheets in Part 2 of this book. Third, to describe a process for evaluating the program.

○ LAYING THE GROUNDWORK

Now that we have looked at the child's developmental stages with regard to literary needs, it is time to take the rich literary heritage of finger games, lullabies, songs, poems, etc., and combine them into a program. All the children's songbooks, finger-game collections, Mother Goose books, and simple picture stories are excellent sources of material. But how to organize and present this literature?

Organizing the Material

It is best to use a formula in constructing program activities. Program themes can create a framework to gather materials together for a baby-toddler event. Themes such as going to school, birthdays, and growing up are rites of passage for both parent and child. There are fifty-two theme-related programs in Part 2 of this book. These demonstrate a variety of possible motifs, from dogs to gardening. Themes are not, however, necessary for successful programs. Thematically unrelated songs, books, and finger games still provide a satisfying and effective experience. When staff members design a program, individuality and personal talents should dictate the format. Above all else, baby-toddler programs should be fun for both the audience and the staff. Many formulas work; these are as personal as the staff who create them. The sample handout sheets incorporated in this book are based on the following structure.

Opening Song: An opening theme song is used every week to set an upbeat mood. The familiar music lets the audience, especially the children, know that it is program time. Very young children learn this song and can sing along, developing a sense of mastery and participation. Select a song that can be enjoyed week after week. Songs like

"The More We Get Together"[1] or "It's a Small World"[2] express universal concepts of togetherness and are popular and well known.

Name Song: Each child's name is incorporated into a song such as "Charlie over the Water."[3] Some staff are wonderful at remembering everyone's name, but asking parents to introduce their child to the group also works. Using names makes for a more personal program, and introduces you and the audience to one another.

Prebook Finger Game: A finger game that ends with hands in the lap prepares the way for the first book. "Open, Shut Them" is a favorite.[4]

Book: Book time is when a young audience will become restless. Choose a book with brief text, a simple plot, and large, colorful illustrations. Encourage participation, especially with a rhyming or repeated text. Get adults and toddlers to repeat phrases together. Babies may crawl and toddlers toddle by, but continue to read and share the book. The song or finger game that follows will recapture lost attention. Reading a book demonstrates to caregivers how to engage their child in a picture-book experience.

Song or Finger Game: A lively song or finger game at this point changes the pace and refocuses the audience's attention.

Second Book: The second book is optional and should be shorter, as attention spans are now waning.

Finger Game or Song: A lullaby can be used at this point to calm and relax the audience. Caregivers often rock the children to the music.

Tickle or Lap Jog: These two activities afford the group the opportunity to move and relax. They also encourage the reuniting of the adult and wandering child for the finale. The librarian can invite one of the children to ride his or her knees.

Ending Song: The ending song should be a lively time with all-out participation. "If You're Happy and You Know It" has become a standard.[5] As with the opening song, the child quickly learns, sings along, and participates. This ends the program on a happy note.

Preparing Activity Sheets

Activity sheets, or handouts, are the heart of the program and serve several important functions. First, they act as a guide for the staff during a program. There have been many times when I couldn't remember the exact words or guitar chords to a song. All I had to do was glance at the handout. Handout sheets save on preparation time because you do not have to memorize everything.

Second, handouts help the audience participate, especially with unfamiliar material. Third, the handouts serve as a learning tool for parents. They are encouraged to take them home and practice the new material with their child. Fourth, handouts serve as a record of what materials and books have been used.

Creating new handouts can be time-consuming. Part 2 of this book provides many examples to get you started. Choose a theme, copy the handout, and select one or two related books either of your own choosing or from the suggested list. Activity sheets can be rearranged to create new and individualized programs. Cut and paste repeated portions such as opening and closing songs, add new material, and copy. Alternatively, enter materials on a computer and compile a new handout when needed. (Note that all handouts should be printed in upper- and lowercase type. All capital letters can be confusing for adults who are just learning to read or the visually impaired.) "Try a rerun once in a while. No one will remember a program done a few months ago, especially if a new book is used."[6] Go ahead and repeat favorite material. Caregivers and children will feel comfortable with a familiar song or finger game. "A successful lapsit is a combination of old and new materials creating a familiar yet exciting program."[7]

The activity sheet's appearance may be enhanced by a graphic. Theme-related pictures, such as a birthday cake or jack-o-lantern, add appeal. Those who are not artists can use clip art or rubber stamp art. If *Spot Goes to School* is the book chosen for a program, try a "Spot" rubber stamp for the corresponding handout.[8] A handout that is attractive is more likely to go home with the family.

Creating the Right Setting

Consider the available programming areas in the library and choose a site conducive to the program. A circle of chairs or rug pieces encourages group participation. A rug on the floor is good for babies to crawl on, and the circle of chairs helps contain them. Brightly colored bins of board books on the floor and a stuffed animal mascot that attends each program create a friendly environment. The optimum setup is next to or in the picture-story area. This can lead to higher circulation, as it makes it easy for the staff to assist in book selection. It also makes the program highly visible to the public. There is nothing better for community relations than a group of very young children in the library.

Programming rooms also work and have the advantage of containing the children and the extra noise. Whatever site is chosen, the size of the audience is a factor. Having a few people in a large area is as unwelcoming as a large group in a tiny area. Match the audience with the area whenever possible, to create a successful event. It has been my experience that between fifteen and thirty people is the optimum audience size.

A book display on a nearby table or shelf assists caregivers with book selection and allows parts of the collection to be highlighted. Multiple copies of the books used in the program can be displayed. Many patrons will want to take home the featured books. New books, parenting books, age-appropriate picture stories, song and finger-game collections, poetry and nursery rhyme collections are all favorites, as are records, audiocassettes, and CDs.

Crayons, paper, and wooden puzzles on a nearby table give toddlers something to do before and after the program, providing adults an opportunity to browse for books.

Scheduling the Programs

Very young children are dependent upon adults, be they parents, foster parents, other family members, baby sitters, or nannies, to bring them to the library. When these caregivers are available and find it convenient to attend will determine the optimum time for a successful program. Assess the community to determine these times. Evening programs will attract working caregivers and other family members such as older siblings. Consider whether patrons feel safe in the area at night. Mornings attract stay-at-home caregivers but may interfere with already existing preschool story times or school class visits. Afternoon programs

are possible, but can interfere with young children's naps and after-school activities in the library. Look at the current patterns of library use. An ideal time for a new program is one when the library is quiet and the audience available. When I moved to the Noe Valley branch of the San Francisco Public Library, it was open until 9 P.M. on Wednesdays, but the children's room was always empty. After the start of a baby-toddler time at 7 P.M., Wednesday nights became very busy. In this case, a population who could attend evening programs turned a slow time into a busy one.

Not all caregivers in an area can attend programs because of time conflicts. When working in a multibranch system, coordination of baby-toddler programs can provide mobile adults with options. A Saturday program may be perfect for a family who could not attend an evening or weekday program. A system-wide flyer listing all the times offered is a must.

Serving Non-English-Speaking Patrons

Many libraries must accommodate parents and children with special language needs. Not every library can provide events in different languages, but referral to branches that can is a good use of available resources. Even if libraries are unable to meet the many language needs of their patrons, it is important to remember that fluency in a language is not necessary for a program with a variety of language elements. Many areas are linguistically and culturally mixed, whereas available, knowledgeable staff is limited. One simple way to integrate non-English materials into a program is to ask a multilingual caregiver who attends the program to teach the staff and audience non-English songs and finger games. Another resource is the paraprofessional library staff, who may have various language abilities. Great benefits can be realized by getting the staff and the audience to work as a team. The main children's department of the San Francisco Public Library has the handouts translated into Chinese and Vietnamese for those caregivers who need them. This way they can also follow along with the English-language program. It is very important to recognize other languages and cultures and preserve all literary heritages.

Serving Children with Disabilities

Presenting books to children with disabilities can be easy if you consult with the caregiver and ask what the child's needs are. You can then make small adjustments. In our group there was a father whose baby daughter had to wear glasses because of severe vision problems. They were seated right in front and I always slowly panned the picture book by her face when reading. I made sure to talk to them before and after the program, standing close so she could see me and connect a face with the voice she heard during the program. The father greatly appreciated these simple considerations. Caregivers of children with disabilities should be encouraged to attend the program. It is good to start babies at baby-toddler programs and mainstream them through life. It is enlightening for the librarian and the other parents and children to discover that all people are different. To reach parents of disabled children, contact the local Easter Seal Society or hospital pediatric clinics. They often have classes and support groups.

With the passage of the Americans with Disabilities Act, public libraries are required to provide interpreters for the deaf upon request. San Francisco is lucky to have a Deaf Services Librarian who is more than willing to provide this service when it has been requested. Good local interpreters can be located by contacting the Registry for Interpreters of the Deaf, Inc., 8719 Colesville Rd., Silver Spring, MD 20910. The telephone number is 301-608-0050. It is extremely important to make all patrons feel welcome by providing these extra considerations and services.

Establishing Policies and Procedures

Some libraries hand out letters to adults discussing what to expect and how to behave at a program. Such a letter suggests the library does not trust the adult and child to behave when they attend the program. If possible, avoid letters altogether. If one is necessary, make it as positive sounding as possible and not a long list of "do nots." Most parents and caregivers are quite aware of what is appropriate child behavior and what is not. Talk privately with an adult whose child is exhibiting disturbing behavior before, during, or after a program. Explain your expectations and why the child is disturbing the rest of the group. This can be an effective way to head off future problems while respecting both the adult and the child.

Sign-up or reservation sheets are common. I always avoided this and on occasion had standing room only. I felt the easy availability of a no-reservation program encouraged patrons who would otherwise not attend. The decision to require reservations is personal and dependent on each individual situation. Some locations might easily draw a hundred patrons for every program. One suggestion might be to offer two programs back to back where large audiences are a regular occurrence.

Name tags are common in toddler and preschool programs. These are not practical with babies, as they like to eat them and the tags are time-consuming to produce and put on. These extras are not necessary for a program to work and they take up valuable time. Consider simplifying whenever possible, and the program will be easier to accomplish and more enjoyable.

Promoting Your Program

Once the commitment is made to provide baby-toddler programming, take steps to make sure your program is well attended. Create an attractive flyer. Approach every adult with a baby or toddler who visits the library, talk up the program, and give them a flyer. Most adults are amazed and pleased to find the library offers an event for their very young child. It makes them feel welcome.

Contact the local preschools and provide them with flyers. Many preschools now have baby and toddler programs and preschoolers often have younger siblings at home. Contact local community centers where adults and children gather, as well as toy and children's clothing stores. Community newspapers can be a wonderful promotional tool, as can local television and radio stations. Get the word out and they will come.

○ SHOW TIME

Now, the stage is set and the audience arrives. Before the program begins, visit with people as they come into the library. Smile and make newcomers welcome. This a great opportunity to get to know young families as you assist them with book selection and reference needs.

Begin the program by personally handing out activity sheets to each adult and any toddler who wants one. Toddlers often will ask for a handout and mimic the adult behavior of reading the sheet during the event. Leave extras for latecomers.

The recommended length of a program is fifteen to twenty-five minutes. Very young children have very short attention spans. Variety and changes of pace are vital to hold this audience. This is why the program should move from fast to slower activities and back again. The librarian should move about, from sitting and reading a book to standing and eliciting audience participation. Make finger games come to life and give the program a dramatic flair whenever possible. The librarian is the catalyst that takes the material on the handout sheet and transforms it into an engaging program. It is important to give the children something to watch.

Most very young children can be noisy and restless. It is the way they are. Young babies tend to be much quieter than their toddler counterparts. They may even fall asleep during the program. Toddlers tend to move about, talk, and sometimes ignore the program in progress. Relax and accept the children's normal behavior as just another part of the baby-toddler time. I remember one program where I was singing and playing the guitar and a baby crawled over and untied my shoelace. Meanwhile, another insisted on helping me play the guitar and a toddler wanted to hand me a book. I smiled at them, sang louder, and the group all laughed at the end. Let the caregivers monitor the children. Remember, getting the adult and child together in the library—not audience control—is the goal. The program's purpose is to foster regular library habits and an acquaintance with new literature.

Finish the program by announcing upcoming library and community events, highlighting new books of special interest, and inviting audience members to make their own announcements or share neighborhood information. A favorite announcement is that of someone's birthday during that week. It is a tradition to sing the birthday song, whether for a child or an adult.

Children enjoy these programs because they can sing and play with other children and adults. Caregivers often report that children demand to come to the programs. Be sure the children feel welcome; a relaxed atmosphere will promote a successful event. The adults are an equally important part of the audience: the children would not be there if not for them. There are many reasons why caregivers return with their child every week. Caregivers confide they feel they are doing something good for their child by learning new materials and, in some cases, learning English. A weekly library visit also provides a time to check out books, meet and talk with friends, and just plain have a good time. Remember that the caregiver is a partner and is necessary for the program to succeed.

○ EVALUATING YOUR PROGRAM

It is important and necessary to evaluate baby-toddler programs and determine whether they are meeting their goals and warrant continued support. This lets you know if you are accomplishing what you planned to do. You must also be prepared to document the success of baby-toddler times, either by formal measurable factors or more casual anecdotal material.

Measurable factors include attendance, circulation, and survey responses. Questionnaires filled out by the program participants are a good way to gather information directly from those you are serving. Figure 1 is a questionnaire adapted from Ellin Greene's wonderful book, *Books, Babies, and Libraries: Serving Infants, Toddlers, Their Parents and Caregivers*.[9] Another modified survey could be sent out to caregivers after children have turned three to monitor the progress of former baby-toddler participants.

Other evidence of the program's results may be anecdotal in nature, including positive comments from participants, letters from the public, and interest from the news media or other libraries. This evidence should be gathered and documented in monthly reports and files that can be produced to justify the program.

Baby-Toddler Program Questionnaire   Date _____

Thank you for taking the time to fill out this questionnaire. Your answers will help plan future programs for you and your child.

Name _____ (optional)

Address _____ (optional)

1. How many children attend the program with you? _____

2. Child/children's ages? _____

3. What is your relationship to the child?   _____ Parent/legal guardian   _____ Other family member
   _____ Babysitter/nanny   _____ Other (please specify) _____

4. Where did you find out about the Baby-Toddler program?   _____ Library flyer/poster   _____ Friend/neighbor
   _____ Other (please specify) _____

5. Is the program day and time convenient for you?   _____ Yes   _____ No
   If no, when would be a better day and time?
   _____ Saturday   _____ Weekday (please specify) _____
   _____ Morning   _____ Afternoon   _____ Evening

6. Did you feel the material was appropriate for the children?
   Books   _____ Very   _____ Somewhat   _____ Not appropriate
   Finger games   _____   _____   _____
   Songs   _____   _____   _____
   Puppets/Felt board   _____   _____   _____
   Film/Video   _____   _____   _____

7. Do you find the program handout sheets helpful during the program?
   _____ Yes   _____ No   _____ Sometimes

8. Do you find it helpful to take the program handout sheets home?   _____ Yes   _____ No   _____ Sometimes

9. How often do you repeat elements from the program at home?
   _____ Often   _____ Sometimes   _____ Never

10. Has your child's interest in books, songs, and finger games changed since attending the program?
    _____ No change   _____ More interested   _____ Less interested

11. Since attending the program, do you spend more time with your child?
    Reading books?   _____ Yes   _____ No
    Singing?   _____ Yes   _____ No
    Doing finger games?   _____ Yes   _____ No

12. Did you have a library card before you began attending the program?   _____ Yes   _____ No

13. Did your child have a library card before you began attending the program?   _____ Yes   _____ No

14. Do you check library materials out when you attend the program?   _____ Yes   _____ No   _____ Sometimes

15. Would you recommend this program to other people with young children?   _____ Yes   _____ No

16. What do you like best about the program?

17. What do you like least about the program?

18. Do you have any suggestions or comments?

Figure 1. ○ Sample questionnaire

Keep in mind your goals and objectives and continue to evaluate the program. If your program attendance is good, if circulation increases, if the staff can handle the extra program and preparation time and the questionnaires are positive, you have a hit on your hands. If things are not all rosy, reevaluate your program times, staff commitment, survey results, publicity, and the need in your community. If the lack of staff time is a problem, perhaps an occasional series of programs would be more manageable than a weekly offering. Maybe more publicity or a change in time would help. Ask yourself if you are reaching the intended audience, and if the programs are lively, fun, and welcoming. Evaluate the strengths and weaknesses and come up with possible solutions.

Notes

1. Tom Glazer, *Eye Winker, Tom Tinker, Chin Chopper: Fifty Musical Fingerplays* (Garden City, N.Y.: Doubleday, 1973), 48.
2. *Illustrated Disney Song Book* (New York: Random House, 1984), 284.
3. Glazer, *Eye Winker,* 18.
4. *Ring a Ring o' Roses: Stories, Games and Finger Plays for Pre-School Children* (Flint, Mich.: Flint Public Library, 1971), 28.
5. Nicki Weiss, *If You're Happy and You Know It: Eighteen Story Songs Set to Pictures* (New York: Greenwillow, 1987), 20.
6. Debby Jeffery and Ellen Mahoney, "Sitting Pretty: Infants, Toddlers and Lapsits," *School Library Journal* 35 (April 1989), 38.
7. Ibid.
8. Books cited are included in the bibliographies unless otherwise noted.
9. Ellin Greene, *Books, Babies and Libraries: Serving Infants, Toddlers, Their Parents and Caregivers* (Chicago: American Library Association, 1991), 133–34.

CHAPTER

3 Tips for Successful Programs

After years of experience programming for babies and toddlers, both personal and secondhand, one learns how to present a program as well as how to teach someone else. There are tricks of the trade that make these programs much easier to do, more successful, and much more enjoyable. This chapter gives advice from how to deal with the fears of the first program to ways to avoid the boredom of presenting a program year after year.

○ SURVIVING YOUR FIRST PROGRAMS

There is something about facing babies, toddlers, and adults that can be intimidating, even to the most seasoned children's librarian. People with years of preschool story times under their belts have expressed fear at facing this group of young children and adults. If the truth be known, in some ways baby-toddler programs can be easier than their preschool counterparts because the caregivers are there to help you.

I vividly remember my first baby-toddler program. I was a new librarian in the main children's department of the San Francisco Public Library, which did not yet have a "Lapsit" program. First, I went to see the program at the Merced branch. Next, I carefully planned the program and practiced the materials to the point where I could have done it in my sleep. Then, I enlisted a partner to assist in the presentation. When the big day came

it brought doubts and an upset stomach. Thankfully, all went well and every program became easier. In a short while it was my favorite program and still is today.

The first few programs will be the hardest because they are new and unfamiliar. Below are some ideas to help assure success and prevent nerve attacks.

See Another Program

Visiting someone else's program can be invaluable. If there is already a program in the library system or geographical area, ask for an invitation to see it. Not only is this proof positive that the program can work, the fun and enjoyment of the audience will be encouraging. This is also a good time to ask for help and support.

Plan Your First Programs Carefully

Plan the first few programs with extra care. Choose easy and familiar books, songs, and finger games to present—perhaps some familiar personal favorites. The program should be memorized and practiced, so that disruptions are not unduly distracting. Practicing in front of a mirror or for a friend can make the first presentation more fluid. One librarian entertained her pets as she mastered the material. This intensive time investment up front will pay off later. The experienced baby-toddler programmer becomes familiar with the format and the audience, making preparation and presentation quick and easy.

Have a Buddy

Use the buddy system if possible. Do the program with one other staff member, be it another children's librarian or a paraprofessional. In the main children's department at the San Francisco Public Library there was a very talented library page, Betty Rose Allen. She could sing, play the autoharp, and remember all the children's names. For years she did team "Lapsits" with many different librarians. Her presence at all the programs gave them continuity as the librarians rotated. She also assisted new librarians in becoming comfortable and familiar with the program and the audience.

Presenters in multibranch systems can help each other out. If there is already a librarian doing baby-toddler programs, ask him or her to assist with your first couple of programs. Being part of a team doing a new program is less fearful than going it alone.

Wear Bright Clothes

Another way to help with the first few programs is to wear clothes that give children something eye-catching to look at. This is personal and dependent upon your wardrobe. Hats, bold jewelry, or brightly colored clothing give the children something to focus on. The librarian also gains confidence and a sense of showmanship.

Use Music in the Program

Librarians who could not carry a tune if it had handles on it, take heart. Go ahead and sing anyway, and the adults will carry the tune. A librarian who just cannot, or will not, sing can be a "rapper," rhythmically saying the verses and clapping along.

A music assistant is another possibility. This can be another staff member, a program attendee, or a volunteer from the community. In this day of small compact disc players and audiotape machines, the librarian can use recorded music and everyone can sing along with the recording, sort of baby-toddler karaoke. Putting music in the program in any form will make for a more attentive and happy group.

○ THE AUDIENCE IS NOT THE ENEMY

Discipline

Very young babies are usually quiet in a library situation. They may watch all the activities going on around them with a fierce concentration, or they may fall asleep. If they are crying the adult caregiver usually removes them. Babies are typically a very attentive audience. Older babies, the crawlers and walkers as well as the toddlers of the group, may go from active participation to active disruption. Let the caregivers deal with serious breaches of program conduct. If they don't, talk to them quietly after the program. The librarian shouldn't have to control the children's behavior, as is necessary in a preschool story time, because the caregivers are present.

Your library may already be experiencing an influx of young children and caregivers coming to use the collection. They bring along baby strollers and diaper bags, blocking aisles and creating congestion. Toddlers carry around juice bottles or crackers despite the library's "no food" policy. Diapers need to be changed and babies will want to nurse. This is part of having young children and babies in a library. All of the above behavior may also happen in the middle of the baby-toddler program. There should not be any hard and fast rules when young children and their caregivers are concerned. Each situation should be politely corrected or blissfully ignored. Baby strollers can be placed in an out-of-the-way place. Diapers are best changed and disposed of in the bathroom. A discretely placed table can be used, but be sure the caregiver disposes of the diaper properly. A smelly diaper does not add to the ambience of the library. Young children need food at regular intervals throughout the day. Bottles of milk or juice and finger foods should be allowed, and nursing mothers politely not seen.

The Caregiver as Partner

Caregivers have a large investment in wanting the program to succeed. They are not critical and want the program to work as much as the librarian does. The librarian and the adult audience have similar goals and are a team. A new baby-toddler programmer should keep this in mind. Caregivers view bringing their child to the library as a positive thing, and it makes them feel good. They come to learn what to read to their child and how to do it. They come because it is fun, develops regular reading habits, and gives the child a head start in reading and socializing. Caregivers also come to be socialized. Caregivers for whom English is a second language come to improve their own language skills. They learn U.S. and European culture along with other cultures presented through books and folklore. Think of caregivers as partners.

Prepare the Library Staff

Young children are noisy and active. For a library staff to commit to this program, it must first accept this. Before, during, and after the program, there will be more people in the library and some of them may be very loud. Public libraries have become more user-friendly over the years. More talking and activity are now allowed, especially where children are concerned. Children and their caregivers should be made to feel welcome and comfortable so they will return.

If you decide to introduce a baby-toddler program to the library, discuss it with the staff first. Talk over library etiquette and listen to the concerns of other librarians and staff. Explain why the programs are so important to both adults and children. Talk up the benefits of such a program to the library. A toddler might sit on top of the checkout desk, chewing rubber bands, while the father checks out books, but the bottom line is often increased circulation for many libraries when budget time rolls around. The Merced branch of San Francisco Public Library reported a 40 percent increase in the children's area after the Lapsit program was begun. Because books for this group are quickly read, caregivers tend to check out many books at one time.

Increased circulation is one result of the program, but it is not the major goal. Children from birth to three years of age have as much right to library services and programs as their preschool counterparts. A library can make reaching out to these youngest patrons part of its mission. Once a library staff appreciates this goal, they will be much more willing to be understanding and supportive of baby-toddler times.

Capitalize on Community Support

Other benefits of baby-toddler programs include the creation of a strong base of community support and a public relations gold mine. Because the adults get to know the staff so well and appreciate the program so much, they will fight very hard for their library. They become involved on a very personal level. If the library is faced with budget problems or staff reductions (as who isn't these days?) this group will come to the rescue. Baby-toddler programs are popular with the media as well. Local newspapers and television stations love covering this beat. It has everything from babies and family values to libraries and reading. The "Lapsits" at San Francisco Public have had numerous wonderful stories reported in the media, including a national piece done by CBS.

○ PRESENTERS' BURNOUT

After doing baby-toddler programs for some time, it may be difficult to remain enthusiastic. Below are some ideas to avoid program burnout.

Add Variety

Variety is the spice of life, and that is certainly true of baby-toddler programs. Always be on the lookout for a new book or other material to use. This can include buying new books for the library collection or using a popular new song from a children's film. Buy a new puppet or musical instrument. Learn a funny song or think up a unique theme for a program. In other words, keep on the lookout for new toys or other program materials. These items will inspire fresh ideas and keep programming a pleasure.

Put extra care into holiday programs, making them special events. Be sure holiday decorations have appeal to young children; add simple crafts or a special performer. Ask adult attendees to bring cookies and juice to be served after the program. Every Halloween I would dress in costume and invite participants to come in costume too. Very young babies made good pumpkins or clowns. Toddlers came as dragons and fairies. By the end of the program, most of the adults carried wings and tails that the children had removed for comfort. Then pumpkin cookies and apple juice were served. This was a favorite program for everyone.

Develop a Support Group

Developing a support group is also helpful for creative inspiration. Get together with others who present similar programs if it is geographically possible. If not, find someone to correspond with. In this way program ideas and materials can be shared, along with funny and not-so-funny experiences. San Francisco Public had an unofficial "Lapsit" committee that met occasionally and did just that. The group always found it useful and beneficial to their spirits as well as to their programs. Support groups help avoid that feeling of isolation, particularly for children's librarians who are often alone at a location.

Take a Break

Librarians should schedule breaks from programs. This allows batteries to recharge and help revitalize the program. If there is more than one children's librarian, rotate the program month by month. If you are alone, schedule a series of programs when the work load is light, or take a month off now and then. I often took a break in the month of June. June was always busy with class visits to advertise the summer reading program and the beginning of that same program. It was also a reasonable explanation to use when asked "Why no Lapsit?" by loyal program fans. (Once families get hooked on this program, they can be demanding.)

These are just a few ideas for the new programmer and the old-timer to assure successful and pleasurable baby-toddler times. Librarians must take care of their own well-being while providing services to young children and their caregivers.

Choosing and Presenting Picture Books

Books are an important element in the baby-toddler program. They introduce both caregiver and child to the wonders of the printed and illustrated page. A child is only young once. That is why books used in the program should be of good quality.

There are many books for babies and toddlers to choose from today, but that was not always so. In the early 1980s, when "Lapsit" programs began at the San Francisco Public Library, there were very few books aimed at the younger audience. There were exceptional books, including the famous *Goodnight Moon* by Margaret Brown, published in 1947.[1] A few years later authors like Donald Crews, Eric Hill, Helen Oxenbury, and Anne and Harlow Rockwell began to write books for younger children that worked well for programming. Even with these, there were never enough. Now there is a large body of books to choose from, which makes programming easier.

○ YOUR SELECTION CRITERIA

When choosing books for baby-toddler programs, be sure the illustrations are good, the text is brief, and the subject age appropriate. Can the book be used in a group setting and do *you* like it? The perfect book for a baby-toddler program might vary from librarian to librarian, but these factors should not.

The Illustrations

Illustrations are extremely important to the young child. The styles will differ but they should always be of superior quality. Large and bright illustrations always help a good programming book. Lois Ehlert's *Feathers for Lunch* gives us beautiful, clean illustrations, easy for a group to see and enjoy. *When You Were a Baby* by Ann Jonas shows large close-up illustrations of familiar everyday objects. On the other hand, *Little Gorilla* by Ruth Bornstein and the *I Hear, I See, I Touch* books by Rachel Isadora have soft lines and colors but the illustrations are still relatively simple. Photographic works like *Whose Hat?* by Margaret Miller or *Mary Had a Little Lamb* by Sarah Hale, with photographs by Bruce McMillan, are also popular with many children. Small books also work, especially if the art work is uncomplicated. A good example of this is *Family,* a board book by Helen Oxenbury. One family member is shown against a white background with his or her name underneath. Simple but wonderful, especially because the last page is "Baby."

Avoid cluttered or complicated illustrations such as *Peek-a-Boo!* by Janet Ahlberg[2] or *Good-Night, Owl* by Pat Hutchins. These books work wonderfully one on one, but are not as effective in a group setting with young children. In the Hutchins book, the animals in the tree cannot be seen clearly from far away, but it makes a wonderful felt board story (see Chapter 6). The Ahlberg book has too many things to see on each page.

The Text

The text is just as important as the illustrations, because text and illustrations must work together to create a quality picture-book experience. The best books for baby-toddler programs have simple texts, from several words to a few lines per page. *Two Bear Cubs* by Ann Jones effectively uses one line of large text per page. A rhyming text is even better, but the rhyme should flow and not be forced. *Ten, Nine, Eight* by Molly Bang has one line per page and a wonderful rhyming text that glides the reader along while the pictures charm. It is a good example of a perfect bedtime story about a father getting his little girl ready for bed.

The Subject

A book might meet the criteria of large, simple, and beautiful illustrations with flowing one line per page text, but if the subject is not interesting to the children and their caregivers the book will not work.

A young child's world is very limited. Several kinds of books seem to appeal. Everyday situations like shopping and preparing a meal can be seen in *Feast for Ten* by Cathryn Falwell. Learning books include Tony Bradman's humorous *Bad Babies' Counting Book* and *How Do I Put It On?* by Shigeo Watanabe. The Donald Crews, Eric Hill, and Harlow Rockwell books take the reader on simple adventures or explore everyday living. *A Rhinoceros Wakes Me Up in the Morning* by Peter Goodspeed teases the imagination with its vivid pictures, rhyming text, and the concept of a child's stuffed animals coming to life.

○ HOW TO CAPTURE THE AUDIENCE

For a successful book experience during a baby-toddler program, the audience must be engaged. This is especially true of the toddler group because they may lose interest and get restless. Even the best librarian doing all the right things with the right book will face occasional restless toddlers. The aim is to keep as many children interested as possible.

The librarian should start with a quality baby-toddler book which she or he really likes. A disliked book should never be shared, as the dislike will come across in some manner even to the baby-toddler group. This goes against the idea of getting them excited about books.

Showing the Pictures

This may sound simple, but the book must be visible to everyone while it is being read. This requires opening the pages W I D E, holding the book away from the body, and swiveling around the group so each person can see, depending on the seating arrangements. Reading upside down or sideways is a very useful skill, with the librarian peering over the top or from the side of the book. The book should be held so that people in the back and the baby on the floor in front can see it. This requires some up-and-down motion as well as swiveling.

Your Read-Aloud Voice

Now that the audience can see the artwork, they also must be able to hear and enjoy the text. The power of the voice is very important to young children from the womb through childhood. Therefore it is important for the librarian to have a good voice for reading aloud. A librarian with a high-pitched voice should practice a lower read-aloud voice. Change the voice to suit the book. If the book is a quiet bedtime story, the reading should be gentle and soft, but loud enough to be heard. If the book rhymes, the meter should be emphasized. When the book is fun or silly, the voice should reflect this with laughter just below the surface. The librarian translates the emotions of the story for the audience with vocal intonations and inflections for a more understandable and enjoyable reading.

Your Pace

The pacing of a reading is very important when sharing a book with an audience. A librarian who tends to speak rapidly should develop a moderate to slow read-aloud pace for successful book reading. Often the book decides much of the timing. Does it rhyme, does it have surprises on every other page or a dramatic ending which requires highlighting? In *Max's First Word*, his sister Ruby tries to get Max to say simple words; all he utters is "BANG." The book steadily builds as Ruby's frustration mounts. The last page has Ruby asking Max to say apple, but instead he says "DELICIOUS," coming to a satisfying, familiar, and funny ending for the baby-toddler group. The last word, "delicious," has to be stressed and the page held open longer than the others to emphasize this ending.

The librarian must develop a personal style that is comfortable but effective in sharing a book. Gentle, quiet styles and energetic presentations seem to work equally well. Both styles include the above-mentioned considerations as well as a love and respect for the audience and the desire to create a satisfying book experience. It is a wonderful feeling when a caregiver and child check out a book just read to them during the program.

○ SHARING HOLIDAYS, LANGUAGES, AND CULTURES

Holiday books help the caregiver and child celebrate together. They introduce holidays and cultures with which other caregivers may not be familiar. Books in other languages are also useful tools. They make children and caregivers of minority cultures feel more comfortable, validating their importance and nourishing the idea that the United States is made up of many different people, a fact that should be celebrated. Using books that share many holidays, languages, and cultures throughout the year impresses upon the caregiver and child that it is a small world after all.

Holidays

Some holidays are more popular with authors and publishers for very young children than others. Christmas, Easter, and Halloween are the favorites. Chanukah and Thanksgiving are gaining in popularity as subjects. These books make holiday programs much easier and enjoyable to do, but other holidays need coverage. What I would not do for a good book on the Chinese New Year, Cinco de Mayo, or Kwanzaa celebrations! The realities are that the publishing industry has long been dominated by European-Americans and there is a European-American bias. Since libraries are a large market, librarians have helped to offset this trend, buying materials about other holidays and cultures, starting up a multi-cultural publishing bandwagon. Small presses specializing in other cultures and languages have sprung up everywhere. Now the task is to become advocates for good quality materials for very young children. Make a statement by spending money on materials that celebrate lesser-known holidays or cultures but are good books in their own right.

Because there is a lack of books about holidays representing non-European cultures, the librarian has to be creative by using books that are not about the holiday, but are related in some way. For Chinese New Year the zodiac animals can be used to create an enjoyable program. 1994 was the year of the dog, which offered a variety of materials to choose from for a "Dog of a New Year." For the less common animals, different zodiac animal songs, finger games, and books may be used. For example, if it is the year of the pig, an enjoyable program might consist of *Pink Pigs in Mud* by Betty Youngs or Nancy Tafuri's *Spots, Feathers and Curly Tails*, combined with finger games like "This Little Pig Went to Market."[3] (See Chinese New Year Activity Sheet.)

Other Languages

It is very difficult to find programming books for very young children in other languages. Eric Hill's "Spot" books have been translated into many other languages, including sign language, but that is an exception. Many times foreign language books are not from major publishers and are difficult to find. (See the Multilingual and Multicultural Resources bibliography.) If you wish to use a book like *¿Donde Está Spot?*, the Spanish translation of *Where's Spot?*, is there anyone on the staff who can read it properly? If not, is there anyone in the audience who can read it? I have read the English version of Hill's book side by side with a Spanish-speaking adult who read the Spanish version. I would read a page and then she would read the same page in Spanish. This technique worked very well. It was a good way to involve a group member as well as provide a satisfying bilingual book experience. A book can be read in another language alone, or translated as the reading progresses, or two books read in tandem as we did. All of the above create a program that is richer and broader in scope. It also validates and welcomes other cultural experiences, whether there are people in the audience who speak the language or not.

Other Cultures

Books that explore other cultures for young children are even rarer than books in other languages. *Jafta* by Hugh Lewin is an exception. In *Jafta*, a small boy in Africa likes to roar like a lion and relate to other wild animals. Though this book is aimed at preschoolers, it can be successfully used in baby-toddler programs. It must be read well and with enthusiasm because of the brown and cream illustrations. In *On Mother's Lap* by Ann Herbert Scott, an arctic mother has enough room on her lap for both her children. *Hats, Hats, Hats* and *Houses and Homes* by Ann Morris show a variety of hats and homes from around the world and the different people who occupy them. There is a need for more books for young children about young children around the world. We can encourage writers and publishers to produce more in the future.

Notes

1. Books cited are included in the bibliographies unless otherwise noted.
2. Janet Ahlberg, *Peek-a-Boo!* (New York: Viking, 1981).
3. *The Real Mother Goose* (New York: Checkerboard Press, 1916, 1944), 35.

CHAPTER 5 Sharing the Folklore Traditions

Old Mother Goose
When she wanted to wander
Would fly through the air
On a very fine gander.[1]

Much of the material used in baby-toddler programs comes from oral or folklore traditions. Nursery rhymes, finger games, lullabies, and songs have been verbally handed down for generations, and have been amusing children from time immemorial.

What are the origins of this oral literature? According to *The Annotated Mother Goose,* many rhymes have cloudy and mysterious pasts.[2] No written source goes further back than King Henry VIII, however certain characters appear to have originated much earlier. The character of Mother Goose herself may have been based on Queen Bertha, the mother of Charlemagne. No matter what the source, rhymes serve many purposes. Some rhymes seem to have been designed simply to entertain baby. Some teach, such as verses on counting or days of the week. Still others are riddles, tongue twisters, reports of actual events, or political satire. A few are even thought to be magic spells, incantations, or weather lore. It was only as recently as the seventeenth and eighteenth centuries that many of the standard works were collected and written down. In the United States these collections are often called "Mother Goose" rhymes, in Great Britain "nursery" rhymes, and in many other parts of Europe "folk" rhymes for children.

No matter the origins or the label that is used, this rich mixture of rhymes is a wonderful way to play with a baby and keep him or her entertained. The caregiver and child grow closer, enjoying the interaction of the rhymes and games. Collections of nursery rhymes should be some of the first books a parent or caregiver uses with a new baby. That is why it is important to include these rhymes in baby-toddler programs and encourage adults to use these materials at home.

Though these ditties are fun for the adult and child, they do more than just amuse. Research shows that they introduce young children to the beginnings of speech, intonation, and phrasing. Babies exposed to literature and words at an early age will acquire lots of words. They will learn how to think well, speak well, and be good listeners. Rhymes such as "Jack and Jill" (RMG, p. 49) or "Old Mother Hubbard" (p. 43) introduce older children to story structure, characterization, and setting. Rhymes such as "Ride a Cock-Horse" (p. 30), with the child bounced on a knee, are exercise programs for the younger set. It is no wonder that this oral tradition has withstood the test of time.

Oral traditions appear in a multitude of forms from little jingles like "Hey, Diddle, Diddle" (p. 60) to more expansive narrative rhymes such as "The House That Jack Built." (p. 68) Yet they all share three basic qualities: rhyme, rhythm, and repetition. They practically roll off the speaker's tongue and delight the child's ear. They can be chanted or sung in the bedroom while caring for a child or amusing a little one while standing in the super-market line. They require no props—not even a book—no visuals, no batteries, etc. Only the sound of the caregiver's voice is needed to provide a relaxing and entertaining experience.

One of the best collections of nursery rhymes for very young children is *This Little Pig Went to Market* by Norah Montgomerie. It has sections on rhymes for babies and toddlers that are useful for caregivers. Librarians will also appreciate this sectional approach. Chapters on foot pats and lap jogs help translate the oral traditions into actual activities to do with baby.

There are many fine general collections, from the classic *The Real Mother Goose* with its many rhymes and old-fashioned, colorful illustrations to a more modern version by Tomie DePaola with fewer rhymes and more illustrations. New collections are always being published, so be on the lookout for new books of rhymes, songs, and poetry. Feel free to change a word, line, or verse if it sounds better to the ear or fits in better with the chosen theme.

○ SHARING NURSERY RHYMES

Nursery rhymes used in baby-toddler programs can be roughly divided into categories according to their use. There are foot pats, lap jogs, tickles, hand claps, rocking, finger counting, and general finger games. By demonstrating the various applications of nursery rhymes during the program, you show caregivers how this wealth of material may be used at home.

Foot Pats

Foot pats are simply rhymes that are chanted or sung while the child's foot is rhythmically tapped. These come in handy during diaper changes or while the child is seated in a lap. Bare feet are best, but doing foot pats with shoes, especially when putting them on, is also satisfying. "Shoe the Colt" (RMG, p. 100) or "Cobbler, Cobbler"[3] are simple poems that involve shoes and are perfect for foot pats. During a program, adults with infants are invited to tap their child's foot. The rest of the audience can clap along.

Lap Jogs

Lap jogs are rhymes that are recited while the child is bounced up and down on a lap or knee. These jogs are very popular at programs and have a wider range of appeal than the foot pat. Babies can be jogged, but a toddler loves nothing better. "To market, to market, to buy a fat pig. Home again, home again, jiggity jig." (RMG, p. 19) is an easy jog to render. There are many traditional rhymes that can be used, the only requirement being a bouncy beat.

New poems can also be very successful, like Jack Prelutsky's "Boing! Boing! Squeak!" It is about a bouncing mouse who comes to visit and won't leave. "*Boing! Boing!* Squeak! *Boing! Boing!* Squeak! A bouncing mouse is in my house, it's been here for a week."[4] During a program a child can be invited by the librarian to sit on his or her lap for an enjoyable and exciting ride. Many times the librarian will find that the audience, both adults and children, will demand an encore.

Tickles

Tickles are a very intimate and pleasurable form of play between a child and caregiver. There are many rhymes that make excellent tickles. "Pussy Cat, Pussy Cat" (RMG, p. 26) and "Hickory, Dickory, Dock!" (p. 125) are often used in programs. Somehow, mice or other small creatures are always running up a child's arm, under the chin, or some other ticklish place. One of my favorite tickles comes from my mother. "A bumblebee comes around the barn, with a bundle of stingers under his arm. Buzzzzzzzz!"[5] The thumb and forefinger are put together and flown about to represent the bee. While buzzing, move in for the "sting." What is nice about this one is the child can be tickled anywhere. Whatever tickle rhymes are learned, there should be some in every caregiver's repertoire.

Hand Claps

The most famous and well-known hand clap has to be "Pat-a-Cake, Pat-a-Cake." (RMG, p. 14) It has all the qualities of a great rhyme and clapping game. It has a catchy rhyme and rhythm, deals with the familiar subject of cooking, and can be personalized with the child's name. Clapping hands is a perfect sharing game between adult and child or an individual and a group. Clapping has broad appeal from the youngest child to the adult who still claps hands to music or to acknowledge something well done. A clapping game, such as "Open, Shut Them," should be included in every program.[6]

Rocking

Rocking is the simple movement of swaying back and forth to a rhythmic rhyme or song. At home a rocking chair is often used, soothing both child and adult. In a program everyone can rock side to side or back and forth depending on what is called for. "Rockabye Baby, on the Tree Top" is the classic in this category.[7] Rocking can also be a part of singing "Did You Ever See a Lassie?"[8] This can be a rollicking period during the program where people see just how far they can lean over without falling. "Did you ever see a lassie go this way and that way? Did you ever see a lassie go this way and that?" Be sure to sing the second verse so the "Laddies" in the audience get their turn.

Finger Counts

There are numerous finger and toe counting games. Only the fingers are used during programs, as most children have on shoes. Even though "This Little Pig Went to Market" (RMG, p. 35) is used with fingers, mention to the audience that toes make nice piggies too. This area of finger-games can help the librarian with theme-related materials. The old "One Little, Two Little, Three Little Indians" can generate many new versions for times of need.[9] It can be "One Little, Two Little, Three Little Pilgrims" for Thanksgiving or "Witches" for Halloween, etc. Please do not use the original words. They have been criticized by library professionals, educators, and Native Americans as depicting a group as objects rather than contemporary people.

Make the finger counts easy to do. Instead of holding up one finger at a time, hold up all ten and point to each one as appropriate. Those with infants can touch each finger in turn, while the toddlers of the group will enjoy the challenge. Finger counting helps the child learn hand coordination and number concepts. It is an easy ac-

tivity for the group to do together. Just keep finger counting as simple as possible by choosing easy rhymes or simplifying others.

General Finger Games

The term "finger games" or "fingerplay" refers to rhymes that have body movement accompaniments. Many rhymes can become finger games and many finger games have become songs. It seems there are a million finger games, and there are many collections of them. Librarians should look in their collection for materials to use. *Eye Winker, Tom Tinker, Chin Chopper* by Tom Glazer is a collection of finger-game songs complete with music and directions on how to execute the finger games. A good collection for caregivers is *Finger Rhymes* by Marc Brown with its colorful illustrations and easy to follow directions.

○ TRADITIONAL SONGS

Traditional songs are an important element in the baby-toddler program. Many of the nursery rhymes were traditionally sung or chanted.[10] This fits in with the early bards and poets, who where keepers and creators of early songs and tales. They usually sang or spoke their works while playing a harp or other musical instrument. One can imagine a group of people bathed in firelight, singing the top ten songs of their day. There is something deep within everyone that enjoys music and singing. There are very few opportunities in modern society for people to gather and sing together. Baby-toddler times provide a venue and carry on the traditional songs.

Lullabies

Lullabies are those songs which soothe and, with luck, put a child to sleep. They are in many ways the most poetic and beautiful of the rhymes. Probably the most famous and best known lullaby from England is "Rockabye Baby."[11] Did women long ago hang their cradles in trees while they worked, or is it a moral tale warning people of the dangers of too much pride and ambition? One thing is certain. It has withstood the test of time and is still used and enjoyed by many today.

Lullabies can add a quieting interval to a baby-toddler program and are highly recommended. For those librarians who enjoy singing and perhaps playing a simple instrument, easy lullabies such as "Hush-a-Bye" or "Hush, Little Baby" can be a highlight of the program.[12] These songs are also invaluable to caregivers of young children. They can sometimes soothe and quiet a child better than a warm bottle or breast. Babies love nothing better than to snuggle next to a loved one's chest and feel the resonance of a lullaby softly sung. Couple this with a rocking motion, and it does not get any better for the adult or child. There are many very good collections of lullabies to share with the adult audience, some with easy accompaniments such as Jane Yolen's *Lullaby Song Book*. Some librarians include a lullaby in each program, to emphasize this valuable form of folklore.

Folk Songs

Many songs used for programming come directly from folklore traditions. These folk songs are sometimes finger games put to music such as "Where Is Thumbkin?", a teaching rhyme, or "London Bridge,"[13] a possible report of an actual event dating back to the eleventh century. The famous English folk song "Mary Had a Little Lamb"[14] was published in *McGuffey's Second Reader,* used in American public schools for fifty years. Other songs like "The Mulberry Bush" tell of days when freshly laundered clothes were draped over bushes to dry.[15]

Early Americans also contributed to the popular folk-song traditions. "Skip to My Lou" is a square-dance tune or dancing game.[16] When singing "She'll Be Coming round the Mountain," a group can really enjoy the overall experience of the melody, words, and activities of pulling back on the reins of those horses, etc.[17] These songs give a baby-toddler programmer infinite materials from which to draw, as well as providing a window to the past.

○ OTHER CULTURES AND LANGUAGES

Literary folk rhymes for children, such as Mother Goose collections, offer a wealth of material to use with babies and toddlers. This large body of work generally had its beginnings in Europe and European America. Some exceptions are the spirituals rooted in the African-American experience. "Swing Low, Sweet Chariot"[18] asks for deliverance from slavery, while "Down by the Riverside"[19] longs for the day when people will "study war no more." They are part of the literary folklore of the United States. They have been learned from parents, grandparents, and loved ones. Such rhymes and songs have no known authors and continue to delight generations of children throughout time. Now is the time to expand this cultural folklore to include other cultures and languages.

A baby-toddler program can truly be an enriching experience when adults from other parts of the globe share the oral traditions of their particular cultural backgrounds. Children benefit from these literary heritages above and beyond Mother Goose. And the best source for these rhymes and songs is often the very audience itself.

Once participants begin to relax and feel comfortable with the librarian and one another, they will be more willing to share their cultural folklore with the group. The experience of the program itself will reawaken adults' memories of songs and rhymes chanted to them by a particular loved one when they were babies and toddlers. Particularly shy adults may prefer to teach the librarian a rhyme or song in private. Then the librarian can demonstrate the piece to the group at the following program. Some baby-toddler programs are structured to offer just this opportunity to share family folklore on a regular, ongoing basis. The handouts come in particularly handy when presenting folklore in various languages. Always be sure to document the various entries so the group will know the origins of the piece, including the contributor's name and the geographical location. Thus, many literary heritages can be passed on to the next generation through programs. Traditions from all over the world can be shared and preserved.

Very young children who attend programs may not be fully cognizant of the full language experience but they certainly prove to be an enthusiastic and appreciative audience. Beginning language structures and sounds are introduced while chanting and crooning poetic rhymes and songs. The foundations of story elements are laid as well as the appreciation of a wide array of characters and settings. Most important, baby-toddler programs strengthen the bonds between caregiver and child and others in the group.

Notes

1. *The Real Mother Goose,* 14. Unless otherwise noted, all nursery rhymes cited are from this book with the page numbers given in parentheses.
2. William S. Baring-Gould and Ceil Baring-Gould, *The Annotated Mother Goose* (New York: Clarkson N. Potter, Inc., 1962), 15–16.
3. *Ring a Ring o' Roses: Stories, Games and Finger Plays for Pre-School Children* (Flint, Mich.: Flint Public Library, 1971), 52.
4. Jack Prelutsky, *New Kid on the Block* (New York: Greenwillow, 1984), 126.
5. There is a similar version in *Ring a Ring o' Roses,* 49.
6. Marion F. Grayson, *Let's Do Fingerplays* (Bridgeport, Conn.: Robert B. Luce, Inc., 1962), 79.
7. Norah Montgomerie, *This Little Pig Went to Market* (New York: Franklin Watts, 1966), 36.
8. *Singing Bee! A Collection of Favorite Children's Songs* (New York: Lothrop, Lee & Shepard, 1982), 96.
9. *Ring a Ring o' Roses,* 54.
10. *Annotated Mother Goose,* 223.
11. *Singing Bee!,* 20.
12. Ibid., 11, 12.
13. Ibid., 29, 105.
14. Ibid., 58.
15. Ibid., 80.
16. Ibid., 90.
17. Ibid., 128.
18. Paul Glass, *Songs and Stories of Afro-Americans* (New York: Grosset & Dunlap, 1971), 26.
19. *Go In and Out the Window: An Illustrated Songbook for Young People* (New York: Metropolitan Museum of Art; Henry Holt, 1987), 33.

CHAPTER 6 Beyond Books

Books of nursery rhymes, songs, finger games, and poetry and picture books are the heart of the baby-toddler program. The addition of other media is highly recommended however, to add spice to an already rich mixture. A musical instrument or a puppet adds depth, diversity, and excitement. It introduces caregivers to the joys of puppets, recorded music, and video titles appropriate for young children. The diversity of media will also help in holding the audience's attention; with young children this is always a plus. Please be sure the materials you use are available for public performances.

○ LIVE MUSIC

The importance of music to baby-toddler programs has already been discussed, but many librarians may not be aware of the variety and ease with which music can be incorporated. Adding a musical instrument or recorded music will make the program much more enjoyable for the audience and lead to a more successful program.

The guitar is the most popular portable musical instrument and the most beautiful accompaniment to the human voice. Even though it may look complicated to the novice, simple guitar playing is easy. Most songs can be accompanied by three easy chords. (A chord is a set of notes played at one time.) The G, D, and A7 or the G, F and C chords are the most popular combinations. Many songbooks come with the chords marked above the words and music. *Singing Bee!* is a wonderful songbook with chord diagrams showing where to place the fingers.[1] It presents each song with lovely illustrations and has a subject index. See if there is a guitar lying around a friend's or relative's closet that you can borrow. I borrowed a guitar from a cousin for Lapsits, and later bought one at a garage sale. I recently gave one to a new librarian who had owned a guitar years ago and wanted to use one in her programs. Many people know how to play this instrument. Find someone who can give you a few pointers, use one of the many lesson books, or take a class at a community college or recreation center.

The autoharp is even simpler to play than the guitar. It is a small stringed harp that lies across the lap, with buttons for each chord. To play a C chord, you simply press the C button and strum the strings. Autoharps need to be tuned by a professional once in a while, and it is difficult to find used ones, but they make it easy to add music to the program.

Rhythm sticks are two pieces of polished wood that are struck together in time for a nice background sound. These can be bought at any music store and are fun for adding that extra beat. Any rhyme or song that lends itself to clapping is a good candidate for rhythm sticks. The foot pat "Cobbler, Cobbler,"[2] or the song "Working on the Railroad,"[3] can remind one of a cobbler or railroad worker hammering away.

Electric keyboards are small enough now to be held on a lap during a program. They can be used for simple chords or more complicated finger work. They are also great for adding sound effects and simple tunes to a book. John Philbrook of the San Francisco Public Library does a wonderful version of Galdone's *The Three Bears*. While reading the book he gives each bear its own chord, with baby bear's way up high. When Goldilocks enters, many notes are hit for a dissonant sound. With the addition of the music, this longer book succeeds in holding the attention of the audience.

Violins, harmonicas, flutes, recorders, and accordions are all possibilities for adding an extra musical element. Librarians should search their musical past and see if it is not time to drag that accordion down from the attic.

Noisemakers can add something special to a particular song or lap jog. They range from kazoos and bells to plastic bottles filled with rice or beans. Small cans can be filled with rattle material and then covered with a cardboard top and wrapped in colorful paper. A tambourine or small drum can be perfect for a rhythmic poem or song. At the Christmas program, I passed out small bells strung on yarn. Everyone rang their bells while we sang "Jingle Bells."[4] Afterwards the children were delighted they could take the bells home.

○ RECORDED MUSIC

Everyone can be invited to sing along to recorded music. Most libraries have a selection of tape or disc formats that require only a small machine to play. Search the collection for appropriate songs that will fit in with program themes and add that little extra for a special event. Several of the titles cited in the list of recorded music have popular songs with singing and music on one side and only the music on the reverse. This allows for great sing-along opportunities.

Recorded Music Sampler

Animaland. Produced by Bumble Buzz Records, 1992. Dist. by Silo, Audiocassette.

Twelve animals are identified in song from the rock 'n' roll "Bumblebeez Theme Song" to "Cows on the Moon." A good theme enhancer for programs.

Bessette, Mimi. *Lullabies of Broadway.* Music for Little People, 1990. Audiocassette or CD.

Songs from popular movies and Broadway musicals, such as "White Christmas," "The Sound of Music," and many more are given the lullaby treatment. Carefully selected and arranged; recommended.

Canten Navidad. Dist. by Multi-Cultural Audio Video Systems. Audiocassette.

Twelve Christmas songs in Spanish from Spain and America. Comes with a song sheet.

A Child's Celebration of Showtunes. Music for Little People, 1992. Audiocassette or CD.

Broadway songs sung by the original performers, such as "My Favorite Things" by Julie Andrews and "Put on a Happy Face" by Dick Van Dyke.

A Child's Celebration of Songs. Music for Little People, 1992. Audiocassette or CD.

A wonderful collection sung by the original performers. Includes "Over the Rainbow" by Judy Garland, Burl Ives doing "Polly Wolly Doodle" and so much more. Highly recommended.

A Child's World of Lullabies: Multicultural Songs for Quiet Time. Educational Activities, 1994. Audiocassette or CD.

Music and songs with a variety of instruments from around the world.

Family Folk Festival: A Multi-Cultural Sing Along. Music for Little People, 1990. Audiocassette and CD.

Celebrating different musical styles, cultures, and folk traditions from all over the Western world come old and new favorites sung by such artists as Pete Seeger, Taj Mahal, and Sweet Honey in the Rock. Includes "Grandfather's Clock" and "I've Been Working on the Railroad."

Fink, Cathy, and Marcy Marxer. *A Cathy and Marcy Collection for Kids.* Rounder Records, 1994. Dist. by Silo. CD.

A compilation of hits from three award-winning recordings. Songs include "Magic Penny," "It's a Beautiful Day," and "Susie and the Alligator."

Herdman, Priscilla. *Daydreamer.* Music for Little People, 1993. Audiocassette or CD.

Thirteen tranquil songs such as "Ticklish Tom and Pickildy Pie."

———. *Star Dreamer: Nightsongs and Lullabies.* Produced by Alacazam!, 1988. Dist. by Music for Little People. Audiocassette or CD.

New and traditional songs with beautiful vocals and instrumental and a flavor of old English folk songs.

Jenkins, Ella. *Counting Games.* Dist. by Afro-Am Distributing Co.

Simple rhythmic counting games including "One, Two, Buckle My Shoe."

———. *Nursery Rhymes.* Dist. by Afro-Am Distributing Co.

Swinging renditions of well-known nursery rhyme favorites such as "Muffin Man" and "Pat-a-Cake."

Joining Hands with Other Lands: Multicultural Songs and Games. Kimbo Educational, 1994. Audiocassette or CD.

Includes such songs as "Chinese New Year," "Many Ways to Say Hello," and more.

Kaldor, Connie, and Carmen Campagne. *Lullaby Berceuse.* Music for Little People, 1988. Audiocassette.

This bilingual French and English collection of original lullabies is an award winner and sure to please.

Les Petits Chanteurs de Paris. Distributed by Multi-Cultural Audio Video Systems. Audiocassette.

The National Boys' Choir of Paris sings French songs for children.

Muldaur, Maria. *On the Sunny Side.* Music for Little People, 1990. Audiocassette or CD.

Familiar songs from the '30s, '40s, and '50s come to life. Includes "Side by Side" and "Would You Like to Swing on a Star?"

Monet, Lisa. *Circle Time: Songs and Rhymes for the Very Young.* Music for Little People, 1989. Audiocassette.

Songs and rhymes that are traditional favorites, "If You're Happy," "The Little Teapot," and more.

Olde Mother Goose. August House, 1993. Audiocassette.

Twenty-one popular and well-produced traditional nursery rhyme songs including "Lavender's Blue" and "Mary Had a Little Lamb."

Palmer, Hap, and Martha Palmer. *Baby Songs.* Educational Activities, 1984. Dist. by Music for Little People. Audiocassette or CD.

The classic "Today I Took My Diaper Off" and other songs celebrate the joys of a child's everyday world.

Peter, Paul and Mommy. Music for Little People, 1992. Original release date in the '70s. Audiocassette or CD.

A classic with tunes like "Going to the Zoo" and "Puff, the Magic Dragon."

Polisar, Barry Louis. *Old Dogs, New Tricks: Barry Louis Polisar Sings about Animals and Other Creatures.* Rainbow Morning Music, 1993. Audiocassette or CD.

A collection of humorous songs from an artist who was popular in the 1970s. Includes "What If a Zebra Had Spots?" and "Our Dog Bernard."

Raffi. *Everything Grows.* A & M Records, 1987. Dist. by Music for Little People. Audiocassette or CD.

Popular songs as well as new ones from different countries.

———. *One Light, One Sun.* Shoreline, 1985. Dist. by Music for Little People. Audiocassette or CD.

Some old favorites and some new songs from around the world.

———. *Singable Songs for the Very Young.* Troubadour Records. Dist. by Music for Little People, 1976. Audiocassette or CD.

Includes "The More We Get Together," "Baa, Baa, Black Sheep," and "Five Little Frogs."

Re-Bops. *Oldies for Kool Kiddies.* Rebop Records. Dist. by Music for Little People, 1991. Audiocassette.

Rock 'n' roll classics come to life, including "Lollipop," "Rockin' Robin," and "Monster Mash."

Rogers, Sally. *At Quiet o'Clock.* Round River, 1993. Dist. by Music for Little People.

Thirteen traditional and original lullabies including "Ride, Ride, Ranke," a Norwegian lap jog.

Smilin' Island of Song. Music for Little People, 1992. Audiocassette or CD.

Combines Afro-Caribbean reggae with American folk and blues for a Jamaican musical feast with Taj Mahal and Cedella Marley Booker. Island stories are also included, but these are aimed at older children.

Sweet Honey in the Rock. *All for Freedom.* Music for Little People, 1991. Audiocassette or CD.

Tickle Tune Typhoon. *Patty-Cakes and Peek-a-Boos.* Dist. by Music for Little People, 1994. Audiocassette.

> Songs and clapping games including "Open, Shut Them," "Clap Your Hands," and "Barnyard Song."

Wee Sing around the World. Price Stern Sloan, 1994. Audiocassette.

> Samples of other cultures and nations with songs from around the globe. It comes with a booklet containing text, music, and basic chords.

Weed, Joe, and Norton Buffalo et al. *Prairie Lullaby.* Highland Records. Dist. by Music for Little People, 1993. Audiocassette or CD.

> Guitar, harmonica, fiddle, and more bring classic western ballads to life, including "Home on the Range" and "Red River Valley."

The World Sings Goodnight: Lullabies of Thirty-Three Cultures Sung in Their Native Tongue. Music for Little People. Audiocassette or CD.

> A moving collection with men, women, and children sharing their lullabies from all over the globe.

Zip-a-Dee-Doo-Dah. Sony Music, 1992. Dist. by Music for Little People. Audiocassette or CD.

> A collection of Disney songs originally recorded in the 1940s and 1950s by artists Dinah Shore, Benny Goodman and Doris Day. Includes "When You Wish upon a Star," "Whistle While You Work," and many more. Recommended.

Producers and Distributors of Recorded Music

Afro-Am Distributing Company. 407 East 25th St., Suite 600, Chicago, IL 60616. 312-791-1611.

August House. Box 3223, Little Rock, AR 72203.

Educational Activities. P.O. Box 392, Freeport, NY 11520. 800-645-3739, 516-223-4666.

Kimbo Educational. 10 N. Third Ave., Box 477, Long Branch, NJ 07740. 800-631-2187.

Multi-Cultural Audio Video Systems. 19785 West 12 Mile Rd., Suite 207, Southfield, MI 48076. 800-567-2220.

Music for Little People. Box 1460, Redway, CA 95560. 800-727-2233.

Price Stern Sloan. 11150 Olympic Blvd., Los Angeles, CA 90064.

Rainbow Morning Music. 2121 Fairland Rd., Silver Spring, MD 20904. 301-384-9207.

Silo. Box 429, Dept. 318, Waterbury, VT 05676. 800-342-0295, 802-244-5178.

○ VIDEOS AND FILMS

Baby-toddler programs held in formal programming areas have the option of using videos and films. There are a few short titles that work well with this young age group. With longer videos and films, use a section no more than five minutes long, otherwise you will lose your audience. Using a visual medium that also contains music is a nice change of pace from books. Some of the videos and films used with preschoolers will work very well in a program. *Rosie's Walk*, with its catchy barnyard tune, would be a wonderful addition to a program devoted to farm animals. *Max's Christmas*, a delightful story based on the book by Rosemary Wells, would be enjoyed during a Christmas program. Both titles are available in film and video formats. (Titles cited are included in the list of videos and films.) Play a song from the *Sesame Street's Twenty-Fifth Anniversary* video such as "Bein' Green" for St. Patrick's Day. The possibilities are endless. Review the library's collection and see if there is anything appropriate for the baby-toddler program. Please be sure you have performance rights for any material used in programming.

Video and Film Sampler

Alligators All Around. Weston Woods. Video and film. 2 min.

> Based on the book *Really Rosie* by Maurice Sendak. A group of alligators dance and sing their way through the alphabet. Music by Carol King.

Baby's Bedtime. Produced by Joshua M. Greene. Lightyear Entertainment, 1989. Dist. by Media Home Entertainment. Video. 27 min.

Judy Collins sings rhymes and poems in an animated background. Adaptation of Kay Chorao's *The Baby's Bedtime Book.*

Baby's Storytime. Lightyear Entertainment, 1989. Dist. by Media Home Entertainment. Video. 28 min.

"The Three Little Pigs" and ten other folktales are told by Arlo Guthrie. Based on Kay Chorao's *The Baby's Storybook.*

Chicken Soup with Rice. Weston Woods. Video and film. 5 min.

From *Really Rosie* by Maurice Sendak. Carol King's music makes learning the months very enjoyable.

Infantastic Lullabies on Video, Vol. 2. V.I.E.W. Video.

Seven classic nursery songs accompanied by animated familiar objects and bright colors.

It's Not Easy Being Green. Jim Henson Video, 1994. Video.

A Muppet sing-along starring Kermit the Frog, Miss Piggy, Fozzie Bear and Gonzo the Great featuring thirteen songs with on-screen lyrics.

Let's Be Friends. Tickle Toon Typhoon, 1989. Video. 50 min.

The Tickle Tune Typhoon troop present a variety of songs from traditional lullabies to rap.

Mama, Do You Love Me? Words, Inc. Available from StoryTime Associates, 1993. Video.

Based on the book by Joosse, an Inuit mother reassures her daughter that she will love her no matter what. The first section of the video follows the book exactly. The second section contains a glossary and background information about the Inuit people. Show only the book portion of the video for baby-toddler programs.

Max's Chocolate Chicken. Weston Woods. Video and film. 5 min.

Based on the book by Rosemary Wells. Max and Ruby both want the prized chocolate chicken. A good Easter title.

Max's Christmas. Weston Woods, 1988. Video and film. 5 min. Also available in Spanish.

Max meets Santa Claus on Christmas Eve in this wonderful animated version of the holiday story.

Noisy Nora. Weston Woods, 1994. Video and film. 6 min.

Based on the book by Rosemary Wells. Everyone in Nora's house is too busy to listen, but Nora makes her presence known.

One Was Johnny. Weston Woods. Video and film. 3 min.

From *Really Rosie* by Maurice Sendak. An amusing counting rhyme with music by Carol King.

Raffi. *Raffi: A Young Children's Concert.* Troubadour Records. Dist. by Music for Little People, 1984. Video.

Raffi in concert playing and singing children's favorites and interacting with the audience.

Rosie's Walk. Weston Woods. Video and film. 5 min. Also available in Spanish.

From the book by Pat Hutchins. Rosie the hen goes for a a walk, never knowing an ill-fated fox is stalking her.

Sesame Street's Twenty-Fifth Anniversary: A Musical Celebration. Random House Home Video. Video.

Old favorites like "Bein' Green," "Rubber Duckie," and "C Is for Cookie."

The Snowy Day. Weston Woods. Video and film. 6 min. Also available in Spanish.

Based on the book by Ezra Jack Keats. A young child enjoys a city snowfall.

Producers and Distributors of Films and Videos

Random House Inc.   400 Hahn Rd., Westminster, MD 21157.

StoryTime Associates. P.O. Box 5185, Englewood, CO 80155. 303-773-0660.

VIEW Video.   34 E. 23rd St., New York, NY 10010. 212-674-5550, FAX 212-979-0266.

Weston Woods.   Weston, CT 06883-1199. 800-243-5020. In Connecticut, call collect 203-226-3355.

○ PUPPETS AND FELT BOARDS

Younger children enjoy all kinds of puppets, just as preschoolers do. Puppets have always been a way for librarians to add three-dimensional characters to a book or bring a finger game to life. I have used a turtle puppet with a retractable head every time the program "Turtles and Friends" was presented. While I read *Turtle Tale* by Frank Asch, the puppet acted out the motions of the turtle in the book. It was helpful, but not necessary, to have a parent or older child help with the puppet. Everyone loves the turtle and plays with it afterwards. *Turtle Tale* has a longer text, but it succeeds because of the puppet.

Felt boards make a wonderful way to present a book you normally can't share with the group because it is too small or too detailed to be seen. A good example of this is *Good-Night, Owl* by Pat Hutchins. It is a simple book with animal sounds and a satisfying ending. Unfortunately for use with a group, the animals in the tree cannot be seen from a distance. Karey Wehner of the San Francisco Public Library found her own solution. She constructed a two-foot-high cardboard tree, covered it with felt, and put a hole in the trunk for the owl. Then she either cut out the animals from a paperback edition or made them, putting Velcro on the back. The story begins with the owl seated in the tree trunk. As each new bird or the squirrel or bees are introduced, it is placed on the tree with everyone making the appropriate sound. They all make so much noise all day that they keep owl awake. When night comes, he flies to the top of the tree screeching and wakes everybody up. Fortunately, Karey lends this out to other librarians. It was great for baby-toddler and preschool programs, and I used it every year. It always received ovations.

Puppet and Felt Board Sampler

Gates, Frieda. *Glove, Mitten, and Sock Puppets.* New York: Walker, 1978.

A very easy guide to making puppets using gloves, etc.

MacLennan, Jennifer. *Simple Puppets You Can Make.* New York: Sterling, 1988.

Finger- and hand-puppet making with many patterns.

Nancy Renfro Studios. P.O. Box 164226, Austin, TX 78716. 800-933-5512.

A fine but expensive collection of puppets. Catalog available.

Rothman, Fran. *Easy-to-Make Puppets and How to Use Them.* Ill. Chizuko Yasuda. Ventura, Calif.: Regal Books, 1985.

Sullivan, Debbie. *Pocketful of Puppets: Activities for the Special Child with Mental, Physical, and Multiple Handicaps.* Ill. Nancy Renfro. Austin, Tex.: Nancy Renfro Studios, 1982.

Though aimed at children with special needs, this is an excellent resource for puppet ideas.

Theatre Works. 2511 NE – 13th St., Portland, OR 97212. 503-282-7610. FAX 503-243-6815.

A collection of puppets by mail order. Free catalog available.

Wright, Lyndie. *Puppets.* Consultant, Henry Pluckrose. Photography by Chris Fairclough. London: Franklin Watts, 1989.

○ CRAFTS

Simple crafts on special occasions add an extra treat to an infant-toddler program. A simple heart for Valentine's Day or a jack-o-lantern for Halloween is appropriate. Remember, the caregiver will be doing most of the craft and the child will be doing most of the chewing and scribbling. The craft should in some way support and enhance the literary experience but please keep in mind that the baby-toddler program is a literature-based event and crafts should only be of secondary importance. A child can do crafts at home or at daycare centers.

○ PERFORMERS

There are performers and other specialists who can simplify and shorten their usual program for a baby-toddler audience. Start with some likely preschool performers and see if anyone is willing. Singers work best because young children already enjoy music.

The most unusual program I ever presented was "Baby Massage" at the Noe Valley branch in San Francisco. Caregivers were asked to bring a towel and everyone sat or lay on the rug. Then the instructor demonstrated different techniques for better health and relaxation. It was a very different kind of program, but it exposed the modern caregivers to some age-old skills of soothing a child through touch. It was enjoyed because of the novelty. Everyone went home satisfied, but looking forward to a "real" Lapsit the next week.

○ **SIGN LANGUAGE**

Librarians who know sign language can incorporate it into their baby-toddler programs very easily. For others, having someone else sign can be an entertaining and learning experience. There are simple songs and games with easy to learn sign-language accompaniment that are similar to finger games. For professional sign-language interpreters, contact the national office of the Registry for Interpreters of the Deaf, Inc. and ask for a current listing of referral agencies in your community. The address and phone number are 8719 Colesville Rd., Silver Spring, MD 20910, 301-608-0050. Including sign language is invaluable if there are hearing impaired caregivers in the audience and it is a requirement if requested under the new Americans with Disablilites Act. It would also introduce the rest of the audience to another means of communication.

○ **BE CREATIVE**

Integrating media beyond books into infant-toddler programs is like adding more vegetables to the soup—it just gets better. The key is to be flexible and creative when planning a program. Share things with other librarians and support each other. As always, while trying new things, plumb the depths of existing talents and skills to develop that personal program style.

Notes

1. All books mentioned are in the bibliographies included in the book unless otherwise noted.
2. *Ring a Ring o' Roses: Stories, Games and Finger Plays for Pre-School Children* (Flint, Mich.: Flint Public Library, 1971), 52.
3. *Singing Bee! A Collection of Favorite Children's Songs* (New York: Lothrop, Lee & Shepard, 1982), 132.
4. Ibid., 150.

Program Activity Sheets

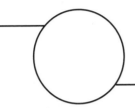

Introduction

If you turned to this part of the book first, you are like I am when I get a new book, wanting to get at the meat right away and dipping into other parts as time goes on. Take note however, that Chapter 2 explains why and how the program sheets are designed and how to get the most out of them.

Part 2 of this book includes fifty-two program sheets with accompanying instruction sheets. Please feel free to use them in any way you wish, from using the program as is to extracting bits and pieces for your own uses. Each instruction sheet has theme-related book suggestions that are included in the annotated bibliography of picture books.

Much of the thematic material can also be used for preschool story times by adding some books for older children. Please note some of the suggested books also work very well with preschool audiences.

Warning: Do not feel forced into thematic programming. Look at the "People Soup" and "Pot-pourri" programs, which are not built around a theme. Donna Trifilo, one of the best baby-toddler programmers I know, does not use themes. I personally like themes and have always used them to hold materials together. No one else should feel bound to do so.

People should make a baby-toddler program their own by personal style and material choices. This book was written as a guide, and I hope will inspire others to program for babies and toddlers. Please remember there are many ways to provide a quality program that is also enjoyable for the programmer as well as the audience. Happy programming.

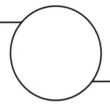

Subject Guide to Activity Sheets

1 My Body, Your Body

Suggested Books

Carlson, *I Like Me*
Gomi, *Everyone Poops*
Holzenthaler, *My Hands Can*
Isadora, *I Hear*
————, *I See*
————, *I Touch*
Martin, *Here Are My Hands*

Opening Song

The More We Get Together

The music is in *Eye Winker, Tom Tinker, Chin Chopper: Fifty Musical Fingerplays* and *The Raffi Singable Songbook*. This song can just be sung or you can add the finger-game aspects.

Verse 1: Hug yourself and sway side to side. Point both fingers to "your friends," then touch yourself on "my friends," then back to hugging.

Verse 2: Clasp hands and sway back and forth. Shake hands with person nearest you, or all hold hands.

Name Song and Finger Game

Charlie over the Water

The music is in *Eye Winker, Tom Tinker . . . .*

Point to everyone for the first two lines. Clap hands on "blackbird," then point to yourself for last line.

Opening Finger Game

Open, Shut Them

Suit actions to words.

Finger Game

Ten Little Fingers

For the first line, wiggle fingers; second line, make a possessive gesture by holding them to your chest. Then follow as directed.

Song

Jack and Jill

The music is in *Singing Bee!*

Song and Finger Game

Eye Winker, Tom Tinker

The music is in *Eye Winker, Tom Tinker . . . .*

Point to eye, ear, nose, mouth, and then tap chin.

Song

Twinkle, Twinkle, Little Star

The music is in *Go In and Out the Window, The Reader's Digest Children's Songbook,* and *Singing Bee!*

Foot Pat

Cobbler, Cobbler, Mend My Shoe

Lightly tap foot along with the rhyme. Others can clap hands.

Closing Song

If You're Happy and You Know It

This well-known song and finger game can be found in *Do Your Ears Hang Low?* or *Ring a Ring o' Roses*. Suit actions to words, clapping and stamping twice, shouting "hooray" once, and repeating them all for "Do all three!"

My Body, Your Body

The More We Get Together

The more we get together, together, together,
The more we get together,
The happier we'll be.

For your friends are my friends
And my friends are your friends.
The more we get together,
The happier we'll be.

The more we share together,
Together, together,
The more we share together,
The happier we'll be.

For sharing is caring and caring is sharing,
The more we share together,
The happier we'll be.

Charlie over the Water

———— over the water,
———— over the sea,
———— catch a blackbird,
Can't catch me!

Open, Shut Them

Open, shut them; open, shut them;
Let your hands go clap, clap, clap.
Open, shut them; open, shut them;
Drop them in your lap, lap, lap.

Walk them, walk them, walk them, walk them,
Right up to your chin, chin, chin.
Open up your little mouth,
But do not let them in.

Book: _____

Ten Little Fingers

I have ten little fingers,
And they all belong to me.
I can make them do things,
Would you like to see?
I can close them up tight,
I can open them wide,
I can hold them up high,
I can hold them down low,
I can wave them to and fro,
And I can hold them just so.

Book: _____

Jack and Jill

Jack and Jill went up the hill,
To fetch a pail of water;
Jack fell down, and broke his crown,
And Jill came tumbling after.

Then up Jack got and off did trot,
As fast he could caper,
To old Dame Dob, who patched his nod
With vinegar and brown paper.

Eye Winker, Tom Tinker

Eye winker, tom tinker,
Nose smeller, mouth eater.
Chin chopper, chin chopper,
Chin chopper, chopper chin.

Twinkle, Twinkle, Little Star

Twinkle, twinkle, little star,
How I wonder what you are,
Up above the world so high,
Like a diamond in the sky.
Twinkle, twinkle, little star,
How I wonder what you are!

Cobbler, Cobbler, Mend My Shoe

Cobbler, cobbler, mend my shoe,
Have it done by half-past two.
Stitch it up and stitch it down,
Now nail the heel all around.

If You're Happy and You Know It

If you're happy and you know it,
 clap your hands.
If you're happy and you know it,
 clap your hands.
If you're happy and you know it,
And you really want to show it,
If you're happy and you know it,
 clap your hands.

Stamp your feet! Shout hooray! Do all three!

2) Let's Get Dressed

Suggested Books

Miller, *Whose Hat?*
———, *Whose Shoe?*
Morris, *Hat, Hats, Hats*
Offen, *A Fox Got My Socks*
Stoeke, *A Hat for Minerva Louise*
Watanabe, *How Do I Put It On?*

Opening Song

The More We Get Together

The music is in *Eye Winker, Tom Tinker* . . . and *The Raffi Singable Songbook.* This song can just be sung or you can add the finger-game aspects.

Verse 1: Hug yourself and sway side to side. Point both fingers to "your friends," then touch yourself on "my friends," then back to hugging.

Verse 2: Clasp hands and sway back and forth. Shake hands with person nearest you, or all hold hands.

Name Song and Finger Game

Charlie over the Water

The music is in *Eye Winker, Tom Tinker* . . . .

Point to everyone for the first two lines. Clap hands on "blackbird," then point to yourself for last line.

Opening Finger Game

Open, Shut Them

Suit actions to words.

Song and Finger Game

This Is the Way We Put on Our Pants

Sung to the tune "The Mulberry Bush." The music is in *Go In and Out the Window* and *Eye Winker, Tom Tinker* . . . .

Pretend to put on each item of clothing letting the actions suit the words.

Song

A-Hunting We Will Go

A traditional song with new words. For each verse, begin with "A-Hunting we will go" and end with "And then we'll let her/them go." The music is in *Singing Bee!*

Tickle

There Came a Little Mouse

Try this tickle from Norway with the English translation. "Mus" is pronounced like "moose."

Creep two fingers up child's arm;
At "But there!" tickle under chin.

Closing Song

If You're Happy and You Know It

This well-known song and finger game can be found in *Do Your Ears Hang Low?* or *Ring a Ring o' Roses.* Suit actions to words, clapping and stamping twice, shouting "hooray" once, and repeating them all for "Do all three!"

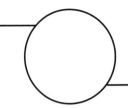

Let's Get Dressed

The More We Get Together
The more we get together, together, together,
The more we get together,
The happier we'll be.

For your friends are my friends
And my friends are your friends.
The more we get together,
The happier we'll be.

The more we share together,
Together, together,
The more we share together,
The happier we'll be.

For sharing is caring and caring is sharing,
The more we share together,
The happier we'll be.

Charlie over the Water
———— over the water,
———— over the sea,
———— catch a blackbird,
Can't catch me!

Open, Shut Them
Open, shut them; open, shut them;
Let your hands go clap, clap, clap.
Open, shut them; open, shut them;
Drop them in your lap, lap, lap.

Walk them, walk them, walk them, walk them,
Right up to your chin, chin, chin.
Open up your little mouth,
But do not let them in.

Book: _____

This Is the Way We Put on Our Pants
This is the way we put on our pants,
Put on our pants, put on our pants,
This the way we put on our pants,
To get dressed in the morning.

This is the way we pull on our socks, . . .
This is the way we tie our shoes, . . .
This is the way we button our top, . . .
This is the way we put on our hat, . . .
This is the way we pull on our coat, . . .
To go to the park in the morning.

Book: _____

A-Hunting We Will Go
A-hunting we will go,
A-hunting we will go,
We'll catch an orange cat,
And give her a hat,
And then we'll let her go.

. . . We'll catch a gray whale,
And give him tie and tails . . .

. . . We'll catch a white goat,
And give him a coat . . .

. . . We'll catch a red fox,
And give him some socks . . .

We'll catch lots you know,
And put them in clothes,
And then we'll let them go.

There Came a Little Mouse
There came a little mouse,
Who would like to find a house.
Not here,
But there!

Kom en liten mus
Som vil gjerne ha et hus
Ikke her, Men der!

If You're Happy and You Know It
If you're happy and you know it,
   clap your hands.
If you're happy and you know it,
   clap your hands.
If you're happy and you know it,
And you really want to show it,
If you're happy and you know it,
   clap your hands.

Stamp your feet! Shout hooray! Do all three!

③ Bedtime

Suggested Books

Bang, *Ten, Nine, Eight*
Berger, *Grandfather Twilight*
Brown, *Goodnight Moon*
Hudson, *Good Night Baby*
Rice, *Goodnight, Goodnight*
Titherington, *Baby's Boat*
Weiss, *Where Does the Brown Bear Go?*

Opening Song

Then More We Get Together

The music is in *Eye Winker, Tom Tinker* . . . and *The Raffi Singable Songbook*. This song can just be sung or you can add the finger-game aspects.

Verse 1: Hug yourself and sway side to side. Point both fingers to "your friends," then touch yourself on "my friends," then back to hugging.

Verse 2: Clasp hands and sway back and forth. Shake hands with person nearest you, or all hold hands.

Name Song and Finger Game

Charlie over the Water

The music is in *Eye Winker, Tom Tinker* . . . .

Point to everyone for the first two lines. Clap hands on "blackbird," then point to yourself for last line.

Opening Finger Game

Open, Shut Them

Suit actions to words.

Song

All the Pretty Little Horses

The music is in *Go In and Out the Window, Singing Bee!* and under a shortened title, "Pretty Little Horses," in *The Baby's Songbook*.

Song

Twinkle, Twinkle, Little Star

The music is in *Go In and Out the Window, The Reader's Digest Children's Songbook* and *Singing Bee!*

Song

Frère Jacques

The music is in *The Baby's Song Book* and *Singing Bee!* This is a traditional French round presented here in English, French, and Spanish.

Lap Jog

Bounce Me

Jog child on lap. Others can clap along.

Closing Song

If You're Happy and You Know It

This well-known song and finger game can be found in *Do Your Ears Hang Low?* or *Ring a Ring o' Roses*. Suit actions to words, clapping and stamping twice, shouting "hooray" once, and repeating them all for "Do all three!"

Bedtime

The More We Get Together

The more we get together, together, together,
The more we get together,
The happier we'll be.

For your friends are my friends
and my friends are your friends.
The more we get together,
The happier we'll be.

The more we share together,
together, together,
The more we share together,
the happier we'll be.

For sharing is caring and caring is sharing,
The more we share together,
the happier we'll be.

Charlie over the Water

————— over the water,
————— over the sea,
————— catch a blackbird,
Can't catch me!

Open, Shut Them

Open, shut them; open, shut them;
Let your hands go clap, clap, clap.
Open, shut them; open, shut them;
Drop them in your lap, lap, lap.

Walk them, walk them, walk them, walk them,
Right up to your chin, chin, chin.
Open up your little mouth,
But do not let them in.

Book: _____

All the Pretty Little Horses

Hushabye, don't you cry
Go to sleep, little baby.
When you wake, you shall have
All the pretty little horses.
Blacks and bays, dapples and grays.
All the pretty little horses.
Hushabye, don't you cry
Go to sleep, little baby.

Book _____

Twinkle, Twinkle, Little Star

Twinkle, twinkle, little star,
How I wonder what you are,
Up above the world so high,
Like a diamond in the sky.
Twinkle twinkle little star,
How I wonder what you are!

Frère Jacques

Are you sleeping, are you sleeping,
Brother John, Brother John?
Morning bells are ringing,
Morning bells are ringing,
Ding, dong, ding! Ding, dong, ding!

Frère Jacques, Frère Jacques,
Dormez vous? Dormez vous?
Sonnez les matines, sonnez les matines,
Don, din, dou! Don, din, dou!

Frey Felipé, Frey Felipé,
¿Duermes tu? ¿Duermes tu?
Toca la campana, toca la campana,
Bam, bam, bam! Bam, bam, bam!

Bounce Me

Bounce me, bounce me,
On your knee.
Bounce me, bounce me,
Pretty please.
Bounce me, bounce me,
Here and there,
Bounce me, bounce me,
Everywhere.

If You're Happy and You Know It

If you're happy and you know it,
    clap your hands.
If you're happy and you know it,
    clap your hands.
If you're happy and you know it,
And you really want to show it,
If you're happy and you know it,
    clap your hands.

Stamp your feet! Shout hooray! Do all three!

4) Food Adventures

Suggested Books

Carle, *Very Hungry Caterpillar*
Degan, *Jamberry*
Shaw, *Sheep out to Eat*
Slobodkinia, *The Wonderful Feast*
Any books listed for the "Let's Eat" or "Happy Birthday" programs.

Opening Song

The More We Get Together

The music is in *Eye Winker, Tom Tinker . . .* and *The Raffi Singable Songbook.* This song can just be sung or you can add the finger-game aspects.

Verse 1: Hug yourself and sway side to side. Point both fingers to "your friends," then touch yourself on "my friends," then back to hugging.

Verse 2: Clasp hands and sway back and forth. Shake hands with person nearest you, or all hold hands.

Name Song and Finger Game

Charlie over the Water

The music is in *Eye Winker, Tom Tinker . . . .*

Point to everyone for the first two lines. Clap hands on "blackbird," then point to yourself for last line.

Opening Finger Game

Open, Shut Them

Suit action to words.

Song

Sing a Song of Sixpence

The music is in *Singing Bee!*

Finger Game

Tortillas, Tortillas

Clap hands pretending to make tortillas while chanting the words.

At "para mi!", touch hands to chest.

Song and Finger Game

She'll Be Coming round the Mountain

The music is in *Singing Bee!, Fireside Book of Fun and Game Songs,* and *Songs America Sings.*

Pretend to pull down on a train whistle;
Wave;
Make a chopping motion against the palm of your hand with the other hand;
Rub your stomach in a circle.

Song

Lullaby and Goodnight

The music is in *The Lullaby Songbook* and *Singing Bee!*

Closing Song

If You're Happy and You Know It

This well-known song and finger game can be found in *Do Your Ears Hang Low?* or *Ring a Ring o' Roses.* Suit actions to words, clapping and stamping twice, shouting "hooray" once, and repeating them all for "Do all three!"

Food Adventures

The More We Get Together

The more we get together, together, together,
The more we get together,
The happier we'll be.

For your friends are my friends
And my friends are your friends.
The more we get together,
The happier we'll be.

The more we share together,
Together, together,
The more we share together,
The happier we'll be.

For sharing is caring and caring is sharing,
The more we share together,
the happier we'll be.

Charlie over the Water

————— over the water,
————— over the sea,
————— catch a blackbird,
Can't catch me!

Open, Shut Them

Open, shut them; open, shut them;
Let your hands go clap, clap, clap.
Open, shut them; open, shut them;
Drop them in your lap, lap, lap.

Walk them, walk them, walk them, walk them,
Right up to your chin, chin, chin.
Open up your little mouth,
But do not let them in.

Book: _____

Sing a Song of Sixpence

Sing a song of sixpence
A pocket full of rye.
Four and twenty blackbirds
Baked in a pie.
When the pie was opened
The birds began to sing.
Wasn't that a
  dainty dish,
To set before
  the king?

Tortillas

Tortillas, tortillas,
Para Mamá,
Tortillas, tortillas,
Para Papá,

Tortillas, tortillas,
Para hermano, (for
brother)
Tortillas, tortillas,
Para mi! (for me)

She'll Be Coming round the Mountain

She'll be coming round the mountain when she
  comes. Toot! Toot!
She'll be coming round the mountain when she
  comes. Toot! Toot!
She'll be coming round the mountain,
She'll be coming round the mountain,
She'll be coming round the mountain when she
  comes. Toot! Toot!

Oh we'll all go out to meet her when she comes.
Hi Babe! . . .

Oh we'll kill the old red rooster when she
comes. Chop! Chop! . . .

Oh we'll all have chicken and dumplings when
she comes. Yum! Yum! . . .

Book: _____

Lullaby and Good Night

Lullaby and good night,
In the sky stars are bright:
Round your head, flowers gay
Scent your slumber till day.
Close your eyes now and rest,
May these hours be blest,
Go to sleep now and rest,
May these hours be blest.

If You're Happy and You Know It

If you're happy and you know it,
  clap your hands.
If you're happy and you know it,
  clap your hands.
If you're happy and you know it,
And you really want to show it,
If you're happy and you know it,
  clap your hands.

Stamp your feet! Shout hooray! Do all three!

5 Let's Eat

Suggested Books

Falwell, *Feast for Ten*
Hayes, *Eat Up, Gemma*
Morris, *Bread, Bread, Bread*
Watanabe, *What a Good Lunch*
Wells, *Max's Breakfast*

Opening Song

The More We Get Together

The music is in *Eye Winker, Tom Tinker . . .* and *The Raffi Singable Songbook.* This song can just be sung or you can add the finger-game aspects.

Verse 1: Hug yourself and sway side to side. Point both fingers to "your friends," then touch yourself on "my friends," then back to hugging.

Verse 2: Clasp hands and sway back and forth. Shake hands with person nearest you, or all hold hands.

Name Song and Finger Game

Charlie over the Water

The music is in *Eye Winker, Tom Tinker . . . .*

Point to everyone for the first two lines. Clap hands on "blackbird," then point to yourself for last line.

Opening Finger Game

Open, Shut Them

Suit action to words.

Song and Finger Game

I'm a Little Teapot

The music is in *Eye Winker, Tom Tinker . . . , Reader's Digest Children's Songbook,* and *Singing Bee!*

Place right hand on hip;
Extend left hand, palm out;
Bend to the left;

Place left hand on hip;
Extend right hand out;
Bend to the right.

Finger Game

Pat-a-Cake, Pat-a-Cake

Clap child's hands together;
Roll them together;
Draw a "B" in palm of child's hand with finger;
Push hands away from body;
Touch hands to chest.

Finger Game

Pease Porridge Hot

Chant or rap while rhythmically clapping to the verse.

Clap lap twice and then
Clap hands together once;
Repeat until rhyme is done.

Song

The Muffin Man

The music is in *Singing Bee!*

Lap Jog

To Market, To Market

Jog child on lap while others clap along.

Closing Song

If You're Happy and You Know It

This well-known song and finger game can be found in *Do Your Ears Hang Low?* or *Ring a Ring o' Roses.* Suit actions to words, clapping and stamping twice, shouting "hooray" once, and repeating them all for "Do all three!"

Let's Eat

The More We Get Together

The more we get together, together, together,
The more we get together,
The happier we'll be.

For your friends are my friends
And my friends are your friends.
The more we get together,
The happier we'll be.

The more we share together,
Together, together,
The more we share together,
The happier we'll be.

For sharing is caring and caring is sharing,
The more we share together,
The happier we'll be.

Charlie over the Water

——— over the water,
——— over the sea,
——— catch a blackbird,
Can't catch me!

Open, Shut Them

Open, shut them; open, shut them;
Let your hands go clap, clap, clap.
Open, shut them; open, shut them;
Drop them in your lap, lap, lap.

Walk them, walk them, walk them, walk them,
Right up to your chin, chin, chin.
Open up your little mouth,
But do not let them in.

Book: _____

I'm a Little Teapot

I'm a little teapot, short and stout,
Here is my handle, here is my spout.
When I get all steamed up, then I shout;
Tip me over and pour me out!

I'm a very clever pot it's true.
Here, let me show you what I can do;
I can change my handle and my spout.
Just tip me over and pour me out!

Pat-a-Cake, Pat-a-Cake

Pat-a-cake, pat-a-cake, baker's man,
Bake me a cake as fast as you can.
Roll it and pat it and mark it with a "B,"
And put it in the oven for baby and me.

Book: _____

Pease Porridge Hot

Pease porridge hot, pease porridge cold,
Pease porridge in the pot, nine days old.

Some like it hot, some like it cold.
Some like it in the pot, nine days old.

The Muffin Man

Oh, do you know the muffin man,
The muffin man, the muffin man?
Oh, do you know the muffin man,
Who lives in Drury Lane?

Oh, yes I know the muffin man, . . .

To Market, To Market

To market, to market, to buy a plum cake;
Home again, home again, market is late.

To market, to market, to buy a plum bun;
Home again, home again, market is done.

If You're Happy and You Know It

If you're happy and you know it,
  clap your hands.
If you're happy and you know it,
  clap your hands.
If you're happy and you know it,
And you really want to show it,
If you're happy and you know it,
  clap your hands.

Stamp your feet! Shout hooray! Do all three!

6 School Days

Suggested Books

Crews, *School Bus*
Hale, *Mary Had a Little Lamb*
  Ill. by DePaola
—————, *Mary Had a Little Lamb*
  Photos by McMillan
Hill, *Spot Goes to School*
Rockwell, *My Nursery School*

Opening Song

The More We Get Together

The music is in *Eye Winker, Tom Tinker . . .* and *The Raffi Singable Songbook.* This song can just be sung or you can add the finger-game aspects.

Verse 1: Hug yourself and sway side to side. Point both fingers to "your friends," then touch yourself on "my friends," then back to hugging.

Verse 2: Clasp hands and sway back and forth. Shake hands with person nearest you, or all hold hands.

Name Song and Finger Game

Charlie over the Water

The music is in *Eye Winker, Tom Tinker . . . .*

Point to everyone for the first two lines. Clap hands on "blackbird," then point to yourself for last line.

Opening Finger Game

Open, Shut Them

Suit action to words.

Song and Finger Game

Wheels on the Bus

The music is in *Eye Winker, Tom Tinker . . .* and *Singing Bee!* under the title "The Bus Song." This popular song usually begins with the "wheels" verse.

Babies are lifted up and down and others can go up and down in their seats;
Roll arms round and round;

Clap one hand against the other;
Open and close hands for the "yak";
Put finger against lips and make "shhh."

Finger Game

One, Two, Three, Four, Five

Hold up one hand and touch each finger;
Clap hands together in front;
Hold up other hand and touch each finger;
Bring hands in front and open wide;
Hold hands together;
Grab little finger with other hand and shake.

Song and Finger Game

This Is the Way We Walk to School

Sung to the tune "The Mulberry Bush" in *Eye Winker, Tom Tinker . . . .*

Move feet; lap jog; make swimming motion;
Pretend to hold a steering wheel; hold arms out to the side.

Song

Mary Had a Little Lamb

The music is in *Singing Bee!* Try showing the book while singing the song.

Tickle

Round and round the Cornfield

Make circles with a finger in the palm of child's hand. Creep fingers up arm and tickle under the chin.

Closing Song

If You're Happy and You Know It

This well-known song and finger game can be found in *Do Your Ears Hang Low?* or *Ring a Ring o' Roses.* Suit actions to words, clapping and stamping twice, shouting "hooray" once, and repeating them all for "Do all three!"

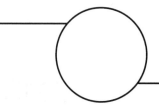

School Days

The More We Get Together

The more we get together, together, together,
The more we get together,
The happier we'll be.

For your friends are my friends
And my friends are your friends.
The more we get together,
The happier we'll be.

The more we share together,
together, together,
The more we share together,
The happier we'll be.

For sharing is caring and caring is sharing,
The more we share together,
The happier we'll be.

Charlie over the Water

————— over the water,
————— over the sea,
————— catch a blackbird,
Can't catch me!

Open, Shut Them

Open, shut them; open, shut them;
Let your hands go clap, clap, clap.
Open, shut them; open, shut them;
Drop them in your lap, lap, lap.

Walk them, walk them, walk them, walk them,
Right up to your chin, chin, chin.
Open up your little mouth,
But do not let them in.

Book: _____

Wheels on the Bus

The children on the bus go up
   and down,
Up and down, up and down.
The children on the bus go up and down,
All through the town.

The wheels on the bus go round and round . . .
The horn on the bus goes beep, beep, beep . . .
The children on the bus go yak, yak, yak . . .
The driver on the bus goes sh, sh, sh . . .

Book: _____

One, Two, Three

One, two, three, four, five,
Once I caught a fish alive.
Six, seven, eight, nine, ten,
But I let him go again.
Why did you let him go?
Because he bit my finger so.
Which finger did he bite?
The littlest finger on the right!

This Is the Way We Walk to School

This is the way we walk to school,
Walk to school, walk to school.
This is the way we walk to school,
So early in the morning.

This is the way we bus to school . . .
This is the way we gallop to school . . .
This is the way we drive to school . . .

Mary Had a Little Lamb

Mary had a little lamb,
Little lamb, little lamb.
Mary had a little lamb,
Its fleece was white as snow.

It followed her to school one day,
School one day, school one day.
It followed her to school one day,
Which was against the rule.

It made the children laugh and play,
Laugh and play, laugh and play.
It made the children laugh and play,
To see a lamb at school.

Round and round the Cornfield

Round and round the cornfield,
Looking for a hare.
Where can we find one? Right up there!

If You're Happy and You Know It

If you're happy and you know it,
   clap your hands.
If you're happy and you know it,
   clap your hands.
If you're happy and you know it,
And you really want to show it,
If you're happy and you know it,
   clap your hands.

Stamp your feet! Shout hooray! Do all three!

7) Let's Play

Suggested Books

Greenfield, *I Make Music*
———, *My Doll, Keshia*
Hill, *Where's Spot?*
Pocock, *Annabelle and the Big Slide*
Raschka, *Yo! Yes?*

Opening Song

The More We Get Together

The music is in *Eye Winker, Tom Tinker . . .* and *The Raffi Singable Songbook.* This song can just be sung or you can add the finger-game aspects.

Verse 1: Hug yourself and sway side to side. Point both fingers to "your friends," then touch yourself on "my friends," then back to hugging.

Verse 2: Clasp hands and sway back and forth. Shake hands with person nearest you, or all hold hands.

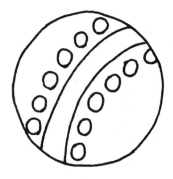

Name Song and Finger Game

Charlie over the Water

The music is in *Eye Winker, Tom Tinker . . . .*

Point to everyone for the first two lines. Clap hands on "blackbird," then point to yourself for last line.

Opening Finger Game

Open, Shut Them

Suit action to words.

Song

London Bridge Is Falling Down

The music is in *The Baby's Song Book, Go In and Out the Window, Reader's Digest Children's Songbook,* and *Singing Bee!* This song may be based on the actual damage or destruction of the bridge in the eleventh century by invading Norsemen. "Hooray" is the modern version of "huzza."

Finger Game

Ten Little Fingers

Hold up ten fingers;
Suit action to words.

Finger Game

Baby's Toys

Form a ball with hands;
Pound one fist on the other;
Clap hands;
Hold up ten fingers;
One fist in front of the other at mouth;
Spread fingers in front of eyes;
Make a roof over head with hands;
Interlock arms and rock them back and forth.

Song

Rockabye Baby

The music is in the *Lullaby Songbook* and *Singing Bee!*

Closing Song

If You're Happy and You Know It

This well-known song and finger game can be found in *Do Your Ears Hang Low?* or *Ring a Ring o' Roses.* Suit actions to words, clapping and stamping twice, shouting "hooray" once, and repeating them all for "Do all three!"

Let's Play

The More We Get Together

The more we get together, together, together,
The more we get together,
The happier we'll be.

For your friends are my friends
And my friends are your friends.
The more we get together,
The happier we'll be.

The more we share together,
Together, together,
The more we share together,
The happier we'll be.

For sharing is caring and caring is sharing,
The more we share together,
The happier we'll be.

Charlie over the Water

——— over the water,
——— over the sea,
——— catch a blackbird,
Can't catch me!

Open, Shut Them

Open, shut them; open, shut them;
Let your hands go clap, clap, clap.
Open, shut them; open, shut them;
Drop them in your lap, lap, lap.

Walk them, walk them, walk them, walk them,
Right up to your chin, chin, chin.
Open up your little mouth,
But do not let them in.

Book: _____

London Bridge Is Falling Down

London Bridge is falling down,
Falling down, falling down,
London Bridge is falling down,
My fair lady.

Build it up with iron and steel, . . .
Iron and steel will bend and bow, . . .
Build it up with wood and clay, . . .
Wood and clay will wash away, . . .

Build it up with stone so strong,
Stone so strong, stone so strong.

Huzza! 'twill last ages long,
My fair lady.

Ten Little Fingers

I have ten little fingers,
And they all belong to me.
I can make them do things,
Would you like to see?

I can close them up tight.
I can open them wide.
I can hold them up high.
I can hold them down low.
I can wave them to and fro,
And I can hold them just so.

Book: _____

Baby's Toys

Here's a ball for Baby,
Big and soft and round;
Here is Baby's hammer,
See how he can pound!
Here are Baby's soldiers,
Standing in a row;
This is Baby's music,
Clapping, clapping so!
Here's a big umbrella,
To keep the baby dry;
Here is Baby's cradle,
To rock a baby bye.

Rockabye Baby

Rockabye baby, on the tree top,
When the wind blows, the cradle will rock;
When the bough breaks, the cradle will fall,
And down will come baby, cradle and all.

If You're Happy and You Know It

If you're happy and you know it,
  clap your hands.
If you're happy and you know it,
  clap your hands.
If you're happy and you know it,
And you really want to show it,
If you're happy and you know it,
  clap your hands.

Stamp your feet! Shout hooray! Do all three!

8 Let's Pretend

Suggested Books

Goodspeed, *A Rhinoceros Wakes Me Up in the Morning*
Lewin, *Jafta*
McPhail, *Pig Pig Rides*

Opening Song

The More We Get Together

The music is in *Eye Winker, Tom Tinker* . . . and *The Raffi Singable Songbook*. This song can just be sung or you can add the finger-game aspects.

Verse 1: Hug yourself and sway side to side. Point both fingers to "your friends," then touch yourself on "my friends," then back to hugging.

Verse 2: Clasp hands and sway back and forth. Shake hands with person nearest you, or all hold hands.

Name Song and Finger Game

Charlie over the Water

The music is in *Eye Winker, Tom Tinker* . . . .

Point to everyone for the first two lines. Clap hands on "blackbird," then point to yourself for last line.

Opening Finger Game

Open, Shut Them

Suit action to words.

Finger Game

Imagine You're an Apple Tree

Stand up;
Reach arms over head;
Let arms begin to droop;
Clap for "Plop" and look down;
Pick up apple and shine it;
Take a bite and rub stomach.

Song

A-Hunting We Will Go

A traditional song with new words. For verses one through five, begin with "A-hunting we will go" and end with "And then we'll let her go."

Closing Song

If You're Happy and You Know It

This well-known song and finger game can be found in *Do Your Ears Hang Low?* or *Ring a Ring o' Roses*. Suit actions to words, clapping and stamping twice, shouting "hooray" once and repeating them all for "Do all three!"

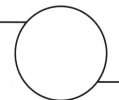

Let's Pretend

The More We Get Together
The more we get together, together, together,
The more we get together,
The happier we'll be.

For your friends are my friends
And my friends are your friends.
The more we get together,
The happier we'll be.

The more we share together,
Together, together,
The more we share together,
The happier we'll be.

For sharing is caring and caring is sharing,
The more we share together,
The happier we'll be.

Charlie over the Water
——— over the water,
——— over the sea,
——— catch a blackbird,
Can't catch me!

Open, Shut Them
Open, shut them; open, shut them;
Let your hands go clap, clap, clap.
Open, shut them; open, shut them;
Drop them in your lap, lap, lap.

Walk them, walk them, walk them, walk them,
Right up to your chin, chin, chin.
Open up your little mouth,
But do not let them in.

Book: _____

Imagine You're an Apple Tree
Imagine you're an apple tree
Growing straight and tall.
Reaching branches toward the sun
With limbs and leaves and all.
And look at all the apples;
They are getting heavy too.
Your branches are getting tired.
Whatever will you do?

Plop! An apple fell off
Pick it up and make it shine
Take a big bite, Yummm!
My, that tasted fine.

Book: _____

A-Hunting We Will Go
A-hunting we will go,
A-hunting we will go,
We'll catch a pink pig
And she'll dance a jig,
And then we'll let her go.

. . . We'll catch a brown bear,
And sit her in a chair, . . .

. . . We'll catch a gray whale,
And pet her big tail, . . .

. . . We'll catch an orange cat,
And feed her till she's fat, . . .

. . . We'll catch a green snake,
And keep him wide awake, . . .

. . . We'll catch a blue bird,
And she'll sing not a word, . . .

A-hunting we will go,
A-hunting we will go,
We'll catch lots of things,
With paws, claws, and wings,
And then we'll let them go.

If You're Happy and You Know It
If you're happy and you know it,
    clap your hands.
If you're happy and you know it,
    clap your hands.
If you're happy and you know it,
And you really want to show it,
If you're happy and you know it,
    clap your hands.

Stamp your feet! Shout hooray! Do all three!

9 Color My World

Suggested Books

Bradman, *Bad Babies' Book of Color*
Carroll, *One Red Rooster*
Charles, *What Am I?*
Crews, *Freight Train*
Goennel, *Colors*
Martin, *Brown Bear, Brown Bear . . .*
Youngs, *Pink Pigs in Mud*

Opening Song

The More We Get Together

The music is in *Eye Winker, Tom Tinker . . .* and *The Raffi Singable Songbook*. This song can just be sung or you can add the finger-game aspects.

Verse 1: Hug yourself and sway side to side. Point both fingers to "your friends," then touch yourself on "my friends," then back to hugging.

Verse 2: Clasp hands and sway back and forth. Shake hands with person nearest you, or all hold hands.

Name Song and Finger Game

Charlie over the Water

The music is in *Eye Winker, Tom Tinker . . . .*

Point to everyone for the first two lines. Clap hands on "blackbird," then point to yourself for last line.

Opening Finger Game

Open, Shut Them

Suit action to words.

Song

Baa, Baa, Black Sheep

A traditional English song. The music is in *Baby's Song Book* and *Singing Bee!*

Song

A-Hunting We Will Go

A traditional song with new words. For verses one through five, begin with "A-hunting we will go" and end with "And then we'll let her/them go." The music is in *Singing Bee!*

Tickle

The Bumblebee

Put forefinger and thumb together for the bee. Fly bee around and then tickle child anywhere at the end of the buzzz!

Closing Song

If You're Happy and You Know It

This well-known song and finger game can be found in *Do Your Ears Hang Low?* or *Ring a Ring o' Roses*. Suit actions to words, clapping and stamping twice, shouting "hooray" once, and repeating them all for "Do all three!"

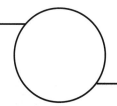

Color My World

The More We Get Together

The more we get together, together, together,
The more we get together,
The happier we'll be.

For your friends are my friends
And my friends are your friends.
The more we get together,
The happier we'll be.

The more we share together,
Together, together,
The more we share together,
The happier we'll be.

For sharing is caring and caring is sharing,
The more we share together,
The happier we'll be.

Charlie over the Water

————over the water,
————over the sea,
————catch a blackbird,
Can't catch me!

Open, Shut Them

Open, shut them; open, shut them;
Let your hands go clap, clap, clap.
Open, shut them; open, shut them;
Drop them in your lap, lap, lap.

Walk them, walk them, walk them, walk them,
Right up to your chin, chin, chin.
Open up your little mouth,
But do not let them in.

Book: _____

Baa, Baa, Black Sheep

Baa, baa, black sheep, have you any wool?
Yes sir, yes sir, three bags full.

One for my master and one for my dame,
And one for the little boy
Who lives down the lane.

Baa, baa, black sheep, have you any wool?
Yes sir, yes sir, three bags full.

Book: _____

A-Hunting We Will Go

A-hunting we will go,
A-hunting we will go,
We'll catch a pink pig,
And she'll dance a jig,
And then we'll let her go.

. . . We'll catch a brown bear,
And sit her in a chair, . . .

. . . We'll catch a gray whale,
And pet her big tail, . . .

. . . We'll catch an orange cat,
And feed her till she's fat, . . .

. . . We'll catch a green snake,
And keep her wide awake, . . .

. . . We'll catch a blue bird,
And she'll sing not a word, . . .

A-hunting we will go,
A-hunting we will go,
We'll catch lots of things,
With paws, claws and wings,
And then we'll let them go.

The Bumblebee

A bumblebee comes around the barn,
With a bundle of stingers under his arm.
Buzzzzzzzzzzzzzzzz!

If You're Happy and You Know It

If you're happy and you know it,
  clap your hands.
If you're happy and you know it,
  clap your hands.
If you're happy and you know it,
And you really want to show it,
If you're happy and you know it,
  clap your hands.

Stamp your feet! Shout hooray! Do all three!

10 Off and Counting

Suggested Books

Bang, *Ten, Nine, Eight*
Blumenthal, *Count-a-Saurus*
Bradman, *Bad Babies' Counting Book*
Bucknell, *One Bear All Alone*
Carle, *One, Two, Three to the Zoo*
Carroll, *One Red Rooster*
Fleming, *Counting*
Gretz, *Teddy Bears 1 to 10*
Noll, *Off and Counting*
Wallwork, *No Dodos*

Opening Song

The More We Get Together

The music is in *Eye Winker, Tom Tinker*... and *The Raffi Singable Songbook*. This song can just be sung or you can add the finger-game aspects.

Verse 1: Hug yourself and sway side to side. Point both fingers to "your friends," then touch yourself on "my friends," then back to hugging.

Verse 2: Clasp hands and sway back and forth. Shake hands with person nearest you, or all hold hands.

Name Song and Finger Game

Charlie over the Water

The music is in *Eye Winker, Tom Tinker* . . . .

Point to everyone for the first two lines. Clap hands on "blackbird," then point to yourself for last line.

Opening Finger Game

Open, Shut Them

Suit action to words.

Finger Game

Ten Little Fingers

For the first line, wiggle fingers; second line, make a possessive gesture by holding them to your chest. Then follow as directed.

Song and Finger Game

Roll Over

This traditional American folk song has many versions.

Hold up ten fingers;
Roll hands over and over;
Now hold up one finger;
Hold up nine fingers;
Now hold up one finger;
Continue to decrease the number of fingers held up until one is left;
At "Good Night!" lean head sideways on folded hands.

Lap Jog

Boing! Boing! Squeak!

This poem by Jack Prelutsky can be found in his collection, *New Kid on the Block*. It also happens to make a great lap jog. This has been a favorite for years among infant-toddler programmers and their audiences. Enjoy.

Jog child on lap. Others can clap along.

Closing Song

If You're Happy and You Know It

This well-known song and finger game can be found in *Do Your Ears Hang Low?* or *Ring a Ring o' Roses*. Suit actions to words, clapping and stamping twice, shouting "hooray" once, and repeating them all for "Do all three!"

Other Suggestions

Songs: "This Old Man" in *Eye Winker, Tom Tinker*... or "The Ants Go Marching" in *Do Your Ears Hang Low?*

Off and Counting

The More We Get Together

The more we get together, together, together,
The more we get together,
The happier we'll be.

For your friends are my friends
And my friends are your friends.
The more we get together,
The happier we'll be.

The more we share together,
Together, together,
The more we share together,
The happier we'll be.

For sharing is caring and caring is sharing,
The more we share together,
the happier we'll be.

Charlie over the Water

———— over the water,
———— over the sea,
———— catch a blackbird,
Can't catch me!

Open, Shut Them

Open, shut them; open, shut them;
Let your hands go clap, clap, clap.
Open, shut them; open, shut them;
Drop them in your lap, lap, lap.

Walk them, walk them, walk them, walk them,
Right up to your chin, chin, chin.
Open up your little mouth,
But do not let them in.

Book: _____

Ten Little Fingers

I have ten little fingers,
And they all belong to me.
I can make them do things,
Would you like to see?
I can hold them up high,
I can hold them down low,
I can wave them to and fro,
And I can hold them just so.

Book: _____

Roll Over

There were ten in the bed,
And the little one said,
"Roll over! Roll over!"
And they all rolled over and one fell out.

There were nine in the bed, . . .
There were eight in the bed, . . .
There were seven in the bed, . . .
There were six in the bed, . . .
There were five in the bed, . . .
There were four in the bed, . . .
There were three in the bed, . . .
There were two in the bed, . . .
There was one in the bed,
And the little one said, "Good night!"

Boing! Boing! Squeak!

Refrain:
Boing! Boing! Squeak!
Boing! Boing! Squeak!
A bouncing mouse is in my house,
It's been here for a week.
It bounced from out of nowhere
Then quickly settled in.
I'm grateful that it came alone
(I've heard it has a twin),
It bounces in the kitchen,
It bounces in the den,
It bounces through the living room—
Look! There it goes again
(Repeat refrain.)

If You're Happy and You Know It

If you're happy and you know it,
  clap your hands.
If you're happy and you know it,
  clap your hands.
If you're happy and you know it,
And you really want to show it,
If you're happy and you know it,
  clap your hands.

Stamp your feet! Shout hooray! Do all three!

11 Growing and Gardening

Suggested Books

Butterworth, *Jasper's Beanstalk*
Ehlert, *Growing Vegetable Soup*
———, *Planting a Rainbow*
Kraus, *The Carrot Seed*
Rockwell, *How My Garden Grew*

Opening Song

I See Daisies

Opening Song

The More We Get Together

The music is in *Eye Winker, Tom Tinker . . .* and *The Raffi Singable Songbook*. This song can just be sung or you can add the finger-game aspects.

Verse 1: Hug yourself and sway side to side. Point both fingers to "your friends," then touch yourself on "my friends," then back to hugging.

Verse 2: Clasp hands and sway back and forth. Shake hands with person nearest you, or all hold hands.

Name Song and Finger Game

Charlie over the Water

The music is in *Eye Winker, Tom Tinker . . . .*

Point to everyone for the first two lines. Clap hands on "blackbird," then point to yourself for last line.

Opening Finger Game

Open, Shut Them

Suit actions to words.

Finger Game

This Is My Garden

Hold hand palm up;
Rake with other hand;
Repeatedly touch with other hand;
Raise hands above head for sun;
Slowly lower wiggling fingers;
Raise both hands with fingers pointed up.

Song

I See Daisies

Sung to the tune "Frère Jacques." Try having one side of the audience start singing the first line. Then start the other side. Rounds are fun, especially if they are sung twice or more.

Song and Finger Game

Eentsy Weentsy Spider

The music is in *Eye Winker, Tom Tinker . . .*

There are several different versions of this finger game. Here is one that works well with very young children.

One hand climbs up arm to shoulder;
Raise hands high and slowly lower them;
Hand slides down arm;
Arms form circle over head;
Hand goes back up to shoulder.

Nursery Rhyme

Mary, Mary, Quite Contrary

Rap or rhythmically say and clap along.

Finger Game

Round and round the Garden

Take palm of child and make a circle with a finger;
Move up arm and tickle under chin.

Closing Song

If You're Happy and You Know It

This well-known song and finger game can be found in *Do Your Ears Hang Low?* or *Ring a Ring o' Roses*. Suit actions to words, clapping and stamping twice, shouting "hooray" once, and repeating them all for "Do all three!"

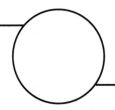

Growing and Gardening

The More We Get Together

The more we get together, together, together,
The more we get together,
The happier we'll be.

For your friends are my friends
And my friends are your friends.
The more we get together,
The happier we'll be.

The more we share together,
Together, together,
The more we share together,
The happier we'll be.

For sharing is caring and caring is sharing,
The more we share together,
The happier we'll be.

Charlie over the Water

———— over the water,
———— over the sea,
———— catch a blackbird,
Can't catch me!

Open, Shut Them

Open, shut them; open, shut them;
Let your hands go clap, clap, clap.
Open, shut them; open, shut them;
Drop them in your lap, lap, lap.

Walk them, walk them, walk them, walk them,
Right up to your chin, chin, chin.
Open up your little mouth,
But do not let them in.

Book: _____

This Is My Garden

This is my garden;
I rake it with care,
And then some flower seeds
I'll plant there.
The sun will shine,
And the rain will fall,
And my garden will blossom
And grow straight and tall.

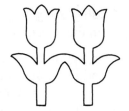

I See Daisies

I see daisies, I see daisies,
Bloom in May, bloom in May.
May's the month for flowers,
Goodbye April showers.
Spring is here, Spring is here.

Book: _____

Eentsy Weentsy Spider

The eentsy weentsy spider
Climbed up the water spout.
Down came the rain
And washed the spider out.
Out came the sun
And dried up all the rain,
And the eentsy weentsy spider
Climbed up the spout again.

Mary, Mary, Quite Contrary

Mary, Mary, quite contrary,
How does your garden grow?
With silver bells and cockle shells,
And pretty maids all in a row.

Round and round the Garden

Round and round the garden,
Went the teddy bear.
One step, two step,
Tickle you under there!

Round and round the garden,
Ran the wee hare.
One jump. Two jumps.
Tickle you under there!

If You're Happy and You Know It

If you're happy and you know it,
    clap your hands.
If you're happy and you know it,
    clap your hands.
If you're happy and you know it,
And you really want to show it,
If you're happy and you know it,
    clap your hands.

Stamp your feet! Shout hooray! Do all three!

12 Weather and Seasons

Suggested Books

Desimimi, *My House*
Florian, *A Summer Day*
———, *A Winter Day*
———, *A Year in the Country*
Stoeke, *A Hat for Minerva Louise*
Wolff, *A Year of Beasts*
———, *A Year of Birds*

Opening Song

The More We Get Together

The music is in *Eye Winker, Tom Tinker* . . . and *The Raffi Singable Songbook*. This song can just be sung or you can add the finger-game aspects.

Verse 1: Hug yourself and sway side to side. Point both fingers to "your friends," then touch yourself on "my friends," then back to hugging.

Verse 2: Clasp hands and sway back and forth. Shake hands with person nearest you, or all hold hands.

Name Song and Finger Game

Charlie over the Water

The music is in *Eye Winker, Tom Tinker* . . . .

Point to everyone for the first two lines. Clap hands on "blackbird," then point to yourself for last line.

Opening Finger Game

Open, Shut Them

Suit actions to words.

Song and Finger Game

Eentsy Weentsy Spider

The music is in *Eye Winker, Tom Tinker* . . .

There are several different versions of this finger game. Here is one that works well with very young children.

One hand climbs up arm to shoulder;
Raise hands high and slowly lower them;
Hand slides down arm;

Arms form circle over head;
Hand goes back up to shoulder.

Finger Game

Rainstorm!!!

Say, "It's starting to rain."
Clap lightly at first;
Clap louder;
Stamp feet for thunder;
Now slowly clap more quietly;
Stop clapping.
Say, "It's stopped raining."

Finger Game

The Little Leaves

Raise hands and lower them, fluttering fingers like falling leaves;
Whirl hands as they flutter;
Touch the floor.

Song

Oh, Susanna

The music is in *Singing Bee!* and *Songs America Sings*.

Finger Game

Baby's Toys

Form a ball with hands;
Pound one fist on the other;
Clap hands;
Hold up ten fingers;
One fist in front of the other at mouth;
Spread fingers in front of eyes;
Make a roof over head with hands;
Interlock arms and rock them back and forth.

Closing Song

If You're Happy and You Know It

This well-known song and finger game can be found in *Do Your Ears Hang Low?* or *Ring a Ring o' Roses*. Suit actions to words, clapping and stamping twice, shouting "hooray" once, and repeating them all for "Do all three!"

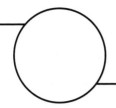

Weather and Seasons

The More We Get Together

The more we get together, together, together,
The more we get together,
The happier we'll be.

For your friends are my friends
And my friends are your friends.
The more we get together,
The happier we'll be.

The more we share together,
Together, together,
The more we share together,
The happier we'll be.

For sharing is caring and caring is sharing,
The more we share together,
The happier we'll be.

Charlie over the Water

—— over the water,
—— over the sea,
—— catch a blackbird,
Can't catch me!

Open, Shut Them

Open, shut them; open, shut them;
Let your hands go clap, clap, clap.
Open, shut them; open, shut them;
Drop them in your lap, lap, lap.

Walk them, walk them, walk them, walk them,
Right up to your chin, chin, chin.
Open up your little mouth,
But do not let them in.

Book: _____

Eentsy Weentsy Spider

The eentsy weentsy spider
Climbed up the water spout.
Down came the rain and
Washed the spider out.
Out came the sun and
Dried up all the rain and
The eentsy weentsy spider
Climbed up the spout again.

Rainstorm!!!

Book: _____

The Little Leaves

The little leaves are falling down,
Round and round, round and round.
The little leaves are falling down,
Falling to the ground.

Oh, Susanna

I come from Alabama
With a banjo on my knee:
I'm going to Lou'siana,
My true love for to see.

It rained all night the day I left,
The weather it was dry;
The sun so hot I froze to death,
Susanna, don't you cry.

Oh, Susanna! Oh don't you cry
    for me,
I come from Alabama
With my banjo on my knee.

Baby's Toys

Here's a ball for Baby,
Big and soft and round;
Here is Baby's hammer,
See how he (she) can pound!
Here are Baby's soldiers,
Standing in a row;
This is Baby's music,
Clapping, clapping so!
Here's a big umbrella
To keep the baby dry;
Here is Baby's cradle,
Rock a baby bye.

If You're Happy and You Know It

If you're happy and you know it,
    clap your hands.
If you're happy and you know it,
    clap your hands.
If you're happy and you know it,
And you really want to show it,
If you're happy and you know it,
    clap your hands.

Stamp your feet! Shout hooray! Do all three!

13 Babies and Toddlers

Suggested Books

Falwell, *We Have a Baby*
Hudson, *Good Morning Baby*
———, *Good Night Baby*
Jonas, *Now We Can Go*
———, *When You Were a Baby*
Ormerod, *To Baby with Love*
Steptoe, *Baby Says*
Wells, *Max's First Word*
Williams, *"More, More, More," Said the Baby*
Wishsky, *Oonga Boonga*

Opening Song

The More We Get Together

The music is in *Eye Winker, Tom Tinker...* and *The Raffi Singable Songbook*. This song can just be sung or you can add the finger-game aspects.

Verse 1: Hug yourself and sway side to side. Point both fingers to "your friends," then touch yourself on "my friends," then back to hugging.

Verse 2: Clasp hands and sway back and forth. Shake hands with person nearest you, or all hold hands.

Name Song and Finger Game

Charlie over the Water

The music is in *Eye Winker, Tom Tinker...*.

Point to everyone for the first two lines. Clap hands on "blackbird," then point to yourself for last line.

Opening Finger Game

Open, Shut Them

Suit actions to words.

Rhyme

What Are Little Boys Made Of?

Rhythmically say or rap this while clapping. It can also be a lap jog.

Song

Lullaby and Good Night

The music is found in *Lullaby Songbook* or *Singing Bee!*

Finger Game

Baby's Toys

Form a ball with your hands;
Pound one fist on the other;
Clap hands;
Hold ten fingers up;
One fist in front of the other at mouth;
Spread fingers in front of eyes;
Make a roof over head with hands;
Interlock arms and rock them back and forth.

Tickle

The Bumblebee

Put forefinger and thumb together for the bee;
Fly bee around and then tickle child anywhere.

Closing Song

If You're Happy and You Know It

This well-known song and finger game can be found in *Do Your Ears Hang Low?* or *Ring a Ring o' Roses*. Suit actions to words, clapping and stamping twice, shouting "hooray" once, and repeating them all for "Do all three!"

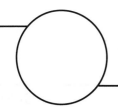

Babies And Toddlers

The More We Get Together

The more we get together, together, together,
The more we get together,
The happier we'll be.

For your friends are my friends
And my friends are your friends.
The more we get together,
The happier we'll be.

The more we share together,
Together, together,
The more we share together,
The happier we'll be.

For sharing is caring and caring is sharing,
The more we share together,
The happier we'll be.

Charlie over the Water

——— over the water,
——— over the sea,
——— catch a blackbird,
Can't catch me!

Open, Shut Them

Open, shut them; open, shut them;
Let your hands go clap, clap, clap.
Open, shut them; open, shut them;
Drop them in your lap, lap, lap.

Walk them, walk them, walk them, walk them,
Right up to your chin, chin, chin.
Open up your little mouth,
But do not let them in.

Book: _____

What Are Little Boys Made Of?

What are little boys made of, made of?
What are little boys made of?
"Snaps and snails, and puppy-dogs' tails;
And that's what little boys are made of."

What are little girls made of, made of?
What are little girls made of?
"Sugar and spice, and all that's nice;
And that's what little girls are made of."

Book: _____

Lullaby and Good Night

Lullaby and good night,
In the sky stars are bright;
Round your head, flowers gay,
Scent your slumbers till day.
Close your eyes now and rest,
May these hours be blest,
Go to sleep now and rest,
May these hours be blest.

Baby's Toys

Here's a ball for Baby,
Big and soft and round;
Here is Baby's hammer,
See how he(she) can pound!
Here are Baby's soldiers,
Standing in a row;
This is Baby's music,
Clapping, clapping so!
Here's a big umbrella
To keep the baby dry;
Here is Baby's cradle,
Rock a baby bye.

The Bumblebee

A bumblebee comes around the barn,
With a bundle of stingers under his arm.
Buzzzzzzzzzzzzzzz!

If You're Happy and You Know It

If you're happy and you know it,
 clap your hands.
If you're happy and you know it,
 clap your hands.
If you're happy and you know it,
And you really want to show it,
If you're happy and you know it,
 clap your hands.

Stamp your feet! Shout hooray! Do all three!

14 Families

Suggested Books

Falwell, *Feast for Ten*
————, *We Have a Baby*
Hill, *Spot's Baby Sister*
Oxenbury, *Family*
Paterson, *Smile for Auntie*
Any books listed for the "Babies and Toddlers" or "Grandma and Grandpa" programs.

Opening Song

The More We Get Together

The music is in *Eye Winker, Tom Tinker* . . . and *The Raffi Singable Songbook*. This song can just be sung or you can add the finger-game aspects.

Verse 1: Hug yourself and sway side to side. Point both fingers to "your friends," then touch yourself on "my friends," then back to hugging.

Verse 2: Clasp hands and sway back and forth. Shake hands with person nearest you, or all hold hands.

Name Song and Finger Game

Charlie over the Water

The music is in *Eye Winker, Tom Tinker* . . . .

Point to everyone for the first two lines. Clap hands on "blackbird," then point to yourself for last line.

Opening Finger Game

Open, Shut Them

Suit actions to words.

Song and Finger Game

¿Donde Está?

Sung to the tune of "Frère Jacques." The music is in *Eye Winker, Tom Tinker* . . . .

Hold up a hand and touch each member of the family when named. For "hermanitos" touch the last three fingers one by one.

Song

Did You Ever See a Lassie?

The music is in *Singing Bee!*

While singing, sway back and forth sideways. Anyone seasick?

Finger Game

This Is My Father

Hold hand up with fingers pointing up.
Point to each member of the family.
Baby is the little finger.
Clasp hands together and hold to chest for last line.

Finger Game

Here Are Grandma's Spectacles

Make circles with thumb and forefinger and hold in front of eyes;
Place hands on head;
Fold hands and put in lap.
Make circles, etc.;
Place hands on head;
Fold arms over chest and sit very straight.

Lap Jogs

This Is the Way the Mothers Ride

Jog children on laps. Others can clap along. On the last line, lift child up on the word "over."

Closing Song

If You're Happy and You Know It

This well-known song and finger game can be found in *Do Your Ears Hang Low?* or *Ring a Ring o' Roses*. Suit actions to words, clapping and stamping twice, shouting "hooray" once, and repeating them all for "Do all three!"

Families

The More We Get Together
The more we get together, together, together,
The more we get together,
The happier we'll be.

For your friends are my friends
And my friends are your friends.
The more we get together,
The happier we'll be.

The more we share together,
Together, together,
The more we share together,
The happier we'll be.

For sharing is caring and caring is sharing,
The more we share together,
The happier we'll be.

Charlie over the Water
——— over the water,
——— over the sea,
——— catch a blackbird,
Can't catch me!

Open, Shut Them
Open, shut them; open, shut them;
Let your hands go clap, clap, clap.
Open, shut them; open, shut them;
Drop them in your lap, lap, lap.

Walk them, walk them, walk them, walk them,
Right up to your chin, chin, chin.
Open up your little mouth,
But do not let them in.

Book: _____

¿Donde Está?
¿Donde está, donde está
Mi familia, mi familia?

Aqui está mamá
Y tambien papá,
Y mis hermanitos,
Y mis hermanitos.

Book: _____

Did You Ever See a Lassie?
Did you ever see a lassie,
A lassie, a lassie?
Did you ever see a lassie,
Go this way and that?
Go this way and that way,
And that way and this way.
Did you ever see a lassie,
Go this way and that?

Did you ever see a laddie, . . .

This Is My Father
This is my father,
This is my mother,
This is my brother,
  tall;
This is my sister,
This is the baby.
Oh! How I love
  them all.

Here Are Grandma's Spectacles
Here are Grandma's spectacles,
And here is Grandma's hat;
And here's the way she folds her hands
And puts them in her lap.

Here are Grandpa's spectacles,
And here is Grandpa's hat;
And here's the way he folds his arms
And sits like that!

This Is the Way the Mothers Ride
This is the way the mothers ride,
Trit trit trot, trit trit trot;

This is the way the fathers ride,
Gallop-a-trot, gallop-a-trot;

And this is the way the babies ride,
Hobbledy-hoy, hobbledy-hoy,
Hobbledy-hobbledy OVER the fence!

If You're Happy and You Know It
If you're happy and you know it,
  clap your hands.
If you're happy and you know it,
  clap your hands.
If you're happy and you know it,
And you really want to show it,
If you're happy and you know it,
  clap your hands.

Stamp your feet! Shout hooray! Do all three!

Grandma and Grandpa

Suggested Books

Berger, *Grandfather Twilight*
Buckley, *Grandfather and I*
——, *Grandmother and I*
Falwell, *Feast for Ten*
Oxenbury, *Family*

Opening Song

The More We Get Together

The music is in *Eye Winker, Tom Tinker . . .* and *The Raffi Singable Songbook*. This song can just be sung or you can add the finger-game aspects.

Verse 1: Hug yourself and sway side to side. Point both fingers to "your friends," then touch yourself on "my friends," then back to hugging.

Verse 2: Clasp hands and sway back and forth. Shake hands with person nearest you, or all hold hands.

Name Song and Finger Game

Charlie over the Water

The music is in *Eye Winker, Tom Tinker . . . .*

Point to everyone for the first two lines. Clap hands on "blackbird," then point to yourself for last line.

Opening Finger Game

Open, Shut Them

Suit actions to words.

Finger Game

Here Are Grandma's Spectacles

Make circles with thumb and forefinger;
Hold in front of eyes;
Place hands on head;
Fold hands and put in lap.
Make circles, etc.;
Fold arms over chest and sit very straight.

Finger Game

Clap Your Hands

Suit action to words.

Song

My Grandma Is Coming to Visit

Sung to the tune "My Bonnie Lies over the Ocean." The music is in *Go In and Out the Window.*

Lap Jog

Ride Away, Ride Away, Baby Shall Ride

Jog child on lap. Others can clap along.

Closing Song

If You're Happy and You Know It

This well-known song and finger game can be found in *Do Your Ears Hang Low?* or *Ring a Ring o' Roses*. Suit actions to words, clapping and stamping twice, shouting "hooray" once, and repeating them all for "Do all three!"

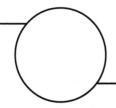

Grandma and Grandpa

The More We Get Together

The more we get together, together, together,
The more we get together,
The happier we'll be.

For your friends are my friends
And my friends are your friends.
The more we get together,
The happier we'll be.

The more we share together,
Together, together,
The more we share together,
The happier we'll be.

For sharing is caring and caring is sharing,
The more we share together,
The happier we'll be.

Charlie over the Water

——— over the water,
——— over the sea,
——— catch a blackbird,
Can't catch me!

Open, Shut Them

Open, shut them; open, shut them;
Let your hands go clap, clap, clap.
Open, shut them; open, shut them;
Drop them in your lap, lap, lap.

Walk them, walk them, walk them, walk them,
Right up to your chin, chin, chin.
Open up your little mouth,
But do not let them in.

Book: _____

Here Are Grandma's Spectacles

Here are Grandma's spectacles,
And here is Grandma's hat;
And here's the way she folds her hands
And puts them in her lap.

Here are Grandpa's
   spectacles,
And here is Grandpa's hat;
And here's the way he folds
   his arms
And sits like that!

Clap Your Hands

Clap your hands, clap your hands,
Clap them just like me.
Touch your knees, touch your knees,
Touch them just like me.
Touch your feet, touch your feet,
Touch them just like me.
Clap your hands, clap your hands,
Now let them quiet be.

Book: _____

My Grandma Is Coming to Visit

My grandma is coming to visit,
My grandma is coming to play.
My grandma is coming to visit,
She's coming to visit today.

Refrain:
Waiting, waiting,
Oh waiting for grandma today, today.
Waiting, waiting,
Oh waiting for grandma today.

We'll go for a walk in the park,
We'll go for a walk at the zoo,
We'll go for a walk in the park,
I hope she will be here soon.
(Repeat refrain.)

My grandpa is coming to visit, . . .

Ride Away, Ride Away, Baby Shall Ride

Ride away, ride away, baby shall ride,
And have a wee puppy dog tied to one side.
A wee pussy cat shall be tied to the other,
And baby shall ride to see her grandmother.

If You're Happy and You Know It

If you're happy and you know it,
   clap your hands.
If you're happy and you know it,
   clap your hands.
If you're happy and you know it,
And you really want to show it,
If you're happy and you know it,
   clap your hands.

Stamp your feet! Shout hooray! Do all three!

16 No Place like Home

Suggested Books

Desimimi, *My House*
Morris, *Houses and Homes*
Rockwell, *In Our House*
Yolen, *Mouse's Birthday*

Opening Song

The More We Get Together

The music is in *Eye Winker, Tom Tinker . . .* and *The Raffi Singable Songbook*. This song can just be sung or you can add the finger-game aspects.

Verse 1: Hug yourself and sway side to side. Point both fingers to "your friends," then touch yourself on "my friends," then back to hugging.

Verse 2: Clasp hands and sway back and forth. Shake hands with person nearest you, or all hold hands.

Name Song and Finger Game

Charlie over the Water

The music is in *Eye Winker, Tom Tinker . . . .*

Point to everyone for the first two lines. Clap hands on "blackbird," then point to yourself for last line.

Opening Finger Game

Open, Shut Them

Suit actions to words.

Song

The Mulberry Bush

The music is in *Singing Bee!*

Here is an old song with new verses. Suit actions to words.

Nursery Rhyme

There Was an Old Lady

Chant or rap rhythmically while clapping along.

Song and Finger Game

Roll Over

Hold up ten fingers. Roll arms around and around. Now hold up one finger. Continue to decrease fingers. At "Good night!" lean head on folded hands.

Tickle

There Came a Little Mouse

Try this finger game from Norway.

Creep two fingers up child's arm;
Tickle under chin.

Closing Song

If You're Happy and You Know It

This well-known song and finger game can be found in *Do Your Ears Hang Low?* or *Ring a Ring o' Roses*. Suit actions to words, clapping and stamping twice, shouting "hooray" once, and repeating them all for "Do all three!"

No Place like Home

The More We Get Together

The more we get together, together, together,
The more we get together,
The happier we'll be.

For your friends are my friends
And my friends are your friends.
The more we get together,
The happier we'll be.

The more we share together,
Together, together,
The more we share together,
The happier we'll be.

For sharing is caring and
  caring is sharing,
The more we share together,
The happier we'll be.

Charlie over the Water

———— over the water,
———— over the sea,
———— catch a blackbird,
Can't catch me!

Open, Shut Them

Open, shut them; open, shut them;
Let your hands go clap, clap, clap.
Open, shut them; open, shut them;
Drop them in your lap, lap, lap.

Walk them, walk them, walk them, walk them,
Right up to your chin, chin, chin.
Open up your little mouth,
But do not let them in.

Book: _____

The Mulberry Bush

Here we go round the mulberry bush,
The mulberry bush, the mulberry bush.
Here we go round the mulberry bush,
So early in the morning.

This is the way we wash our clothes . . .
This is the way we iron our clothes . . .
This is the way we mend our clothes . . .
This is the way we scrub the floors . . .
This is the way we sweep the house . . .

Book: _____

There Was an Old Lady

There was an old lady
Who lived in a shoe.
She had lots of children
So they were crowded too.
She gave them all dinner
With butter and bread.
And read them all stories
And put them to bed.

Roll Over

There were ten in the bed
And the little one said,
"Roll over! roll over!"
So they all rolled over
And one fell out.

There were nine in the bed . . .
. . . Eight . . . Seven . . . Six . . . Five . . .
. . . Four . . . Three . . . Two . . .
There was one in the bed,
And the little one said, "Good night!"

There Came a Little Mouse

There came a little mouse
Who would like to find a house.
Not here,
But there!

Kom en liten mus
Som vil gjerne ha et hus.
Ikke her,
Men der!

If You're Happy and You Know It

If you're happy and you know it,
  clap your hands.
If you're happy and you know it,
  clap your hands.
If you're happy and you know it,
And you really want to show it,
If you're happy and you know it,
  clap your hands.

Stamp your feet! Shout hooray! Do all three!

17 Cars

Suggested Books

Burningham, *Mr. Gumpy's Motor Car*
Florian, *An Auto Mechanic*
Rockwell, *Cars*
Shaw, *Sheep in a Jeep*

Opening Song

The More We Get Together

The music is in *Eye Winker, Tom Tinker . . .* and *The Raffi Singable Songbook.* This song can just be sung or you can add the finger-game aspects.

Verse 1: Hug yourself and sway side to side. Point both fingers to "your friends," then touch yourself on "my friends," then back to hugging.

Verse 2: Clasp hands and sway back and forth. Shake hands with person nearest you, or all hold hands.

Name Song and Finger Game

Charlie over the Water

The music is in *Eye Winker, Tom Tinker . . . .*

Point to everyone for the first two lines. Clap hands on "blackbird," then point to yourself for last line.

Opening Finger Game

Open, Shut Them

Suit actions to words.

Song and Finger Game

Wheels on the Car

Sung to the tune "The Bus Song." The music is in *Eye Winker, Tom Tinker . . .* and *Singing Bee!*

Roll arms for wheels;
Lift child up and down while others can go up and down in their seats;
Clap one hand against the other;
Move arms back and forth like wipers;
Open and close hands for "wah."

Finger Game

Fold Your Hands

Fold hands in front of you;
Lay them in lap;
Pick up book and show it.

Song

This Car

Sung to the tune "This Train."

The music is in *Eye Winker, Tom Tinker . . . .*

Foot Pat

Cobbler, Cobbler, Mend My Shoe

Lightly tap foot along with the rhyme;
Others can clap along.

Closing Song

If You're Happy and You Know It

This well-known song and finger game can be found in *Do Your Ears Hang Low?* or *Ring a Ring o' Roses.* Suit actions to words, clapping and stamping twice, shouting "hooray" once, and repeating them all for "Do all three!"

Cars

The More We Get Together

The more we get together, together, together,
The more we get together,
The happier we'll be.

For your friends are my friends
And my friends are your friends.
The more we get together,
The happier we'll be.

The more we share together,
Together, together,
The more we share together,
The happier we'll be.

For sharing is caring and caring is sharing,
The more we share together,
The happier we'll be.

Charlie over the Water

———— over the water,
———— over the sea,
———— catch a blackbird,
Can't catch me!

Open, Shut Them

Open, shut them; open, shut them;
Let your hands go clap, clap, clap.
Open, shut them; open, shut them;
Drop them in your lap, lap, lap.

Walk them, walk them, walk them, walk them,
Right up to your chin, chin, chin.
Open up your little mouth,
But do not let them in.

Book: _____

Wheels on the Car

The wheels on the car go round and round,
Round and round, round and round,
The wheels on the car go round and round,
All through the town.

The people in the car go up and down, . . .
The horn on the car goes, beep, beep, beep, . . .
The wipers on the car go swish, swish,
  swish, . . .
The baby in the car goes wah, wah, wah, . . .

Fold Your Hands

Fold your hands so quietly,
Fold your hands like this you see.
Ready for a special look?
I'm going to read a special book.

Book: _____

This Car

This car belongs to Daddy, this car,
This car belongs to Daddy, this car,
This car belongs to Daddy,
If he races, Daddy is baddy,
This car belongs to Daddy, this car.

This car belongs to Mommy, this car,
This car belongs to Mommy, this car,
This car belongs to Mommy,
It shines like a penny when it's sunny,
This car belongs to Mommy, this car.

This car belongs to Baby, this car,
This car belongs to Baby, this car,
This car belongs to Baby,
Don't let it fall in the gravy,
This car belongs to Baby, this car.

Cobbler, Cobbler, Mend My Shoe

Cobbler, Cobbler, mend my shoe,
Have it done by half past two.
Stitch it up and stitch it down,
Now nail the heel all around.

If You're Happy and You Know It

If you're happy and you know it,
  clap your hands.
If you're happy and you know it,
  clap your hands.
If you're happy and you know it,
And you really want to show it,
If you're happy and you know it,
  clap your hands.

Stamp your feet! Shout hooray! Do all three!

18 Boats Afloat

Suggested Books

Allen, *Who Sank the Boat?*
Burningham, *Mr. Gumpy's Outing*
Crews, *Harbor*
Rockwell, *Boats*
Shaw, *Sheep on a Ship*

Opening Song

The More We Get Together

The music is in *Eye Winker, Tom Tinker* . . . and *The Raffi Singable Songbook.* This song can just be sung or you can add the finger-game aspects.

Verse 1: Hug yourself and sway side to side. Point both fingers to "your friends," then touch yourself on "my friends," then back to hugging.

Verse 2: Clasp hands and sway back and forth. Shake hands with person nearest you, or all hold hands.

Name Song and Finger Game

Charlie over the Water

The music is in *Eye Winker, Tom Tinker* . . . .

Point to everyone for the first two lines. Clap hands on "blackbird," then point to yourself for last line.

Opening Finger Game

Open, Shut Them

Suit actions to words.

Song

My Bonnie Lies over the Ocean

The music is in *Go In and Out the Window.*

Sway side to side while singing this one. Anyone seasick?

Finger Game

One, Two, Three, Four, Five

Hold up one hand and touch each finger;
Clap hands together in front;
Hold up other hand and touch each finger;
Bring hands in front and open wide;
Hold hands together;
Grab little finger with other hand and shake.

Song

Michael Row the Boat Ashore

The music is in *Songs America Sings.*

Song and Finger Game

Row, Row, Row Your Boat

The music is in *Reader's Digest Children's Songbook* and *Singing Bee!*

Make rowing motions. Try having one side of the audience start singing the first line. Then start the other side. Rounds are fun, especially if the verse is sung twice or more.

Closing Song

If You're Happy and You Know It

This well-known song and finger game can be found in *Do Your Ears Hang Low?* or *Ring a Ring o' Roses.* Suit actions to words, clapping and stamping twice, shouting "hooray" once, and repeating them all for "Do all three!"

Boats Afloat

The More We Get Together

The more we get together, together, together,
The more we get together,
The happier we'll be.

For your friends are my friends
And my friends are your friends.
The more we get together,
The happier we'll be.

The more we share together,
Together, together,
The more we share together,
The happier we'll be.

For sharing is caring and caring is sharing,
The more we share together,
The happier we'll be.

Charlie over the Water

——— over the water,
——— over the sea,
——— catch a blackbird,
Can't catch me!

Open, Shut Them

Open, shut them; open, shut them;
Let your hands go clap, clap, clap.
Open, shut them; open, shut them;
Drop them in your lap, lap, lap.

Walk them, walk them, walk them, walk them,
Right up to your chin, chin, chin.
Open up your little mouth,
But do not let them in.

Book: _____

My Bonnie Lies over the Ocean

My Bonnie lies over the ocean,
My Bonnie lies over the sea,
My Bonnie lies over the ocean,
Please bring back my Bonnie to me.

Refrain:
Bring back, bring back,
Oh, bring back my Bonnie to me, to me.
Bring back, bring back,
Oh, bring back my Bonnie to me.

Oh, blow ye winds over the ocean,
And blow ye winds over the sea,
Oh, blow ye winds over the ocean,
And bring back my Bonnie to me.
(Repeat refrain.)

One, Two, Three

One, two, three, four, five,
Once I caught a fish alive.
Six, seven, eight, nine, ten.
Then I let him go again.
Why did you let him go?
Because he bit my finger so.
Which finger did he bite?
The littlest finger on the right!

Book: _____

Michael Row the Boat Ashore

Michael row the boat ashore, hallelujah.
Michael row the boat ashore, hallelujah.

Sister help to trim the sail, hallelujah.
Sister help to trim the sail, hallelujah.

Jordan's River is deep and wide, hallelujah.
Milk and honey on the other side, hallelujah.
(Repeat first verse.)

Row, Row, Row Your Boat

Row, row, row your boat,
Gently down the stream.
Merrily, merrily, merrily, merrily,
Life is but a dream.

If You're Happy and You Know It

If you're happy and you know it,
    clap your hands.
If you're happy and you know it,
    clap your hands.
If you're happy and you know it,
And you really want to show it,
If you're happy and you know it,
    clap your hands.

Stamp your feet! Shout hooray! Do all three!

19 Trains

Suggested Books

Carle, *One, Two, Three to the Zoo*
Crews, *Freight Train*
Siebert, *Train Song*

Opening Song

The More We Get Together

The music is in *Eye Winker, Tom Tinker* . . . and *The Raffi Singable Songbook*. This song can just be sung or you can add the finger-game aspects.

Verse 1: Hug yourself and sway side to side. Point both fingers to "your friends," then touch yourself on "my friends," then back to hugging.

Verse 2: Clasp hands and sway back and forth. Shake hands with person nearest you, or all hold hands.

Name Song and Finger Game

Charlie over the Water

The music is in *Eye Winker, Tom Tinker* . . . .

Point to everyone for the first two lines. Clap hands on "blackbird," then point to yourself for last line.

Opening Finger Game

Open, Shut Them

Suit actions to words.

Song

This Train Is Chugging Uphill

Sung to the tune "This Train." The music is in *Eye Winker, Tom Tinker* . . . .

Finger Game

This Little Train Went to New York

Touch fingers in sequence starting with thumb; Pull little finger for "Toot."

Song

I've Been Working on the Railroad

The origins of this song are obscure. It probably started out as a minstrel tune. Today it is a popular camping song. The music is in *Go In and Out the Window, Reader's Digest Children's Songbook,* and *Songs America Sings*.

Closing Song

If You're Happy and You Know It

This well-known song and finger game can be found in *Do Your Ears Hang Low?* or *Ring a Ring o' Roses*. Suit actions to words, clapping and stamping twice, shouting "hooray" once, and repeating them all for "Do all three!"

Trains

The More We Get Together

The more we get together, together, together,
The more we get together,
The happier we'll be.

For your friends are my friends
And my friends are your friends.
The more we get together,
The happier we'll be.

The more we share together,
Together, together,
The more we share together,
The happier we'll be.

For sharing is caring and caring is sharing,
The more we share together,
The happier we'll be.

Charlie over the Water

———— over the water,
———— over the sea,
———— catch a blackbird,
Can't catch me!

Open, Shut Them

Open, shut them; open, shut them;
Let your hands go clap, clap, clap.
Open, shut them; open, shut them;
Drop them in your lap, lap, lap.

Walk them, walk them, walk them, walk them,
Right up to your chin, chin, chin.
Open up your little mouth,
But do not let them in.

Book: _____

This Train Is Chugging Uphill

This train is chugging uphill, this train.
This train is chugging uphill, this train.
Through a tunnel, round a bend,
When will this trip ever end?
This train is chugging uphill, this train.

This train is flying downhill, this train.
This train is flying downhill, this train.
This train is flying downhill,
Oh boy, what a thrill!
This train is flying downhill, this train.

This train arrives at the station, this train.
This train arrives at the station, this train.
Slowly, we come to a stop,
Grab our luggage and off we hop.
This train arrives at the station, this train.

Book: _____

I've Been Working on the Railroad

I've been working on the railroad
All the live long day.
I've been working on the railroad,
Just to pass the time away.
Don't you hear the whistle blowing?
Rise up so early in the morn;
Don't you hear the captain shouting,
Dinah blow your horn.

Dinah won't you blow, Dinah won't you blow,
Dinah won't you blow your horn?
Dinah won't you blow, Dinah won't you blow,
Dinah won't you blow your horn?

Someone's in the kitchen with Dinah,
Someone's in the kitchen I know.
Someone's in the kitchen with Dinah,
Strumming on the old banjo.

Fe fi fiddle e-i-o, fe fi fiddle e-i-o,
Fe fi fiddle e-i-o,
Strumming on the old banjo.

If You're Happy and You Know It

If you're happy and you know it,
 clap your hands.
If you're happy and you know it,
 clap your hands.
If you're happy and you know it,
And you really want to show it,
If you're happy and you know it,
 clap your hands.

Stamp your feet! Shout hooray! Do all three!

20 City and Country

Suggested Books

Crews, *Parade*
Helen, *Bus Stop*
Rice, *Goodnight, Goodnight*
Any books listed for the "On the Farm" or
"By the Sea" programs.

Opening Song

The More We Get Together

The music is in *Eye Winker, Tom Tinker . . .* and
The Raffi Singable Songbook. This song can just
be sung or you can add the finger-game aspects.

Verse 1: Hug yourself and sway side to side.
Point both fingers to "your friends," then touch
yourself on "my friends," then back to hugging.

Verse 2: Clasp hands and sway back and forth.
Shake hands with person nearest you, or all
hold hands.

Name Song and Finger Game

Charlie over the Water

The music is in *Eye Winker, Tom Tinker . . . .*

Point to everyone for the first two lines. Clap
hands on "blackbird," then point to yourself for
last line.

Opening Finger Game

Open, Shut Them

Suit actions to words.

Song

The Sidewalks of New York

The music is in *Songs America Sings.*

Song and Finger Game

Wheels on the Bus

The music is in *Eye Winker, Tom Tinker . . .* and
Singing Bee! under the title "The Bus Song."

Roll arms for wheels;
Lift child up and down while others can go up
    and down in their seats;
Clap one hand against the other;
Move arms back and forth like wipers;
Open and close hands for "wah."

Song

The Farmer in the Dell

The music is in *Go In and Out the Window* and
Singing Bee!

Lap Jog

This Is the Way the Ladies Ride

Jog child on lap while others clap along;
Lift up child on last line.

Closing Song

If You're Happy and You Know It

This well-known song and finger game can be
found in *Do Your Ears Hang Low?* or *Ring a Ring
o' Roses.* Suit actions to words, clapping and
stamping twice, shouting "hooray" once, and
repeating them all for "Do all three!"

City and Country

The More We Get Together
The more we get together, together, together,
The more we get together,
The happier we'll be.

For your friends are my friends
And my friends are your friends.
The more we get together,
The happier we'll be.

The more we share together,
Together, together,
The more we share together,
The happier we'll be.

For sharing is caring and caring is sharing,
The more we share together,
The happier we'll be.

Charlie over the Water
———— over the water,
———— over the sea,
———— catch a blackbird,
Can't catch me!

Open, Shut Them
Open, shut them; open, shut them;
Let your hands go clap, clap, clap.
Open, shut them; open, shut them;
Drop them in your lap, lap, lap.

Walk them, walk them, walk them, walk them,
Right up to your chin, chin, chin.
Open up your little mouth,
But do not let them in.

Book: _____

The Sidewalks of New York
East side, West side,
All around the town,
The tots sang ring-a-rosie,
London Bridge is falling down.
Boys and girls together,
Me and Mamie O'Rourke,
Tripped the light fantastic
On the sidewalks of New York.

Wheels on the Bus
The wheels on the bus go round and round,
Round and round, round and round.
The wheels on the bus go round and round,
All around the town.

The people on the bus go up and down, . . .
The horn on the bus goes beep, beep, beep, . . .
The wipers on the bus go swish, swish,
    swish, . . .
The babies on the bus go wah, wah, wah, . . .

Book: _____

The Farmer in the Dell
The farmer in the dell, the farmer in the dell,
Heigh-ho the derry-o, the farmer in the dell.
The farmer takes a wife, . . .
The wife takes a child, . . .
The child takes a nurse, . . .
The nurse take a dog, . . .
The dog takes a cat, . . .
The cat takes a rat, . . .
The rat takes the cheese, . . .
The CHEESE stands alone, . . .

This Is the Way the Ladies Ride
This is the way the ladies ride,
Trit trit trot, trit trit trot!

This is the way the gentlemen ride,
Gallop-a-trot! Gallop-a-trot!

This is the way the farmers ride,
Hobbledy-hoy, Hobbledy-hoy!
Hobbledy hoy OVER the fence!

If You're Happy and You Know It
If you're happy and you know it,
    clap your hands.
If you're happy and you know it,
    clap your hands.
If you're happy and you know it,
And you really want to show it,
If you're happy and you know it,
    clap your hands.

Stamp your feet! Shout hooray! Do all three!

21 By the Sea

Suggested Books

Florian, *Beach Day*
Koch, *By the Sea*
Oxenbury, *Tom and Pippo on the Beach*
Weiss, *Sun, Sand, Sea, Sail*
Any books listed for the "Boats Afloat" program.

Opening Song

The More We Get Together

The music is in *Eye Winker, Tom Tinker* . . . and *The Raffi Singable Songbook*. This song can just be sung or you can add the finger-game aspects.

Verse 1: Hug yourself and sway side to side. Point both fingers to "your friends," then touch yourself on "my friends," then back to hugging.

Verse 2: Clasp hands and sway back and forth. Shake hands with person nearest you, or all hold hands.

Name Song and Finger Game

Charlie over the Water

The music is in *Eye Winker, Tom Tinker* . . . .

Point to everyone for the first two lines. Clap hands on "blackbird," then point to yourself for last line.

Opening Finger Game

Open, Shut Them

Suit actions to words.

Song

Row, Row, Row Your Boat Gently in the Bay

Sung to the tune "Row, Row, Row Your Boat." The music is in *Reader's Digest Children's Songbook* and *Singing Bee!* This makes a good round. Try having half the audience sing the first sentence then begin the other half and sing all three verses. Have fun.

Song

Mary Had a Little Dog

Sung to the tune (you guessed it) of "Mary Had a Little Lamb." Also try "Blow the Man Down," "Blow Ye Winds in the Morning" or "My Bonnie Lies over the Ocean."

Poem

I Found a Pretty Sea Shell

Chant or rap the words;
Where appropriate, hold fist up to ear.

Closing Song

If You're Happy and You Know It

This well-known song and finger game can be found in *Do Your Ears Hang Low?* or *Ring a Ring o' Roses*. Suit actions to words, clapping and stamping twice, shouting "hooray" once, and repeating them all for "Do all three!"

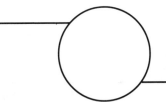

By the Sea

The More We Get Together

The more we get together, together, together,
The more we get together,
The happier we'll be.

For your friends are my friends
And my friends are your friends.
The more we get together,
The happier we'll be.

The more we share together,
Together, together,
The more we share together,
The happier we'll be.

For sharing is caring and caring is sharing,
The more we share together,
The happier we'll be.

Charlie over the Water

——— over the water,
——— over the sea,
——— catch a blackbird,
Can't catch me!

Open, Shut Them

Open, shut them; open, shut them;
Let your hands go clap, clap, clap.
Open, shut them; open, shut them;
Drop them in your lap, lap, lap.

Walk them, walk them, walk them, walk them,
Right up to your chin, chin, chin.
Open up your little mouth,
But do not let them in.

Book: _____

Row, Row, Row Your Boat Gently in the Bay

Row, row, row your boat
Gently in the bay.
Merrily, merrily, merrily, merrily,
What a beautiful day.

Row, row, row your boat
In the deep blue sea.
Merrily, merrily, merrily, merrily,
Life is but a breeze.

Row, row, row your boat,
Now here comes a storm.
Hurrily, hurrily, hurrily, hurrily,
Time to head for home.

Book: _____

Mary Had a Little Dog

Mary had a little dog,
Little dog, little dog.
Mary had a little dog,
His hair was white as snow.

And everywhere that Mary went,
Mary went, Mary went,
And everywhere that Mary went,
The dog was sure to go.

He followed her to the beach one day,
Beach one day, beach one day.
He followed her to the beach one day
And swam in the tide pools.

The dog and Mary laughed and played,
Laughed and played, laughed and played,
The dog and Mary laughed and played,
As they swam in the water cool.

I Found a Pretty Sea Shell

I found a pretty sea shell
And held it to my ear.
I heard the roaring ocean
I heard it very clear.
It had such pretty colors
I took it home with me.
And anytime I want to
I hear the roaring sea.

If You're Happy and You Know It

If you're happy and you know it,
  clap your hands.
If you're happy and you know it,
  clap your hands.
If you're happy and you know it,
And you really want to show it,
If you're happy and you know it,
  clap your hands.

Stamp your feet! Shout hooray! Do all three!

22 Going Places

Suggested Books

Florian, *At the Zoo*
Helen, *Bus Stop*
Hill, *Spot Goes to the Circus*
Norworth. *Take Me Out to the Ballgame*

Opening Song

The More We Get Together

The music is in *Eye Winker, Tom Tinker* . . . and *The Raffi Singable Songbook*. This song can just be sung or you can add the finger-game aspects.

Verse 1: Hug yourself and sway side to side. Point both fingers to "your friends," then touch yourself on "my friends," then back to hugging.

Verse 2: Clasp hands and sway back and forth. Shake hands with person nearest you, or all hold hands.

Name Song and Finger Game

Charlie over the Water

The music is in *Eye Winker, Tom Tinker* . . . .

Point to everyone for the first two lines. Clap hands on "blackbird," then point to yourself for last line.

Opening Finger Game

Open, Shut Them

Suit actions to words.

Song and Finger Game

The Bear Went over the Mountain

The music is in *Eye Winker, Tom Tinker* . . . and *Singing Bee!*

Climb hand up arm;
Shade eyes with hand and look around;
Climb hand down arm;
Look around again on last line.

Song

Take Me Out to the Ballgame

The music is in *Best Loved Songs and Hymns*.

Song

Down by the Station

The music is in *Eye Winker, Tom Tinker* . . . and *Singing Bee!*

Lap Jog

To Market, To Market

Jog child on lap;
Others can clap along.

Closing Song

If You're Happy and You Know It

This well-known song and finger game can be found in *Do Your Ears Hang Low?* or *Ring a Ring o' Roses*. Suit actions to words, clapping and stamping twice, shouting "hooray" once, and repeating them all for "Do all three!"

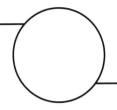

Going Places

The More We Get Together

The more we get together, together, together,
The more we get together,
The happier we'll be.

For your friends are my friends
And my friends are your friends.
The more we get together,
The happier we'll be.

The more we share together,
Together, together,
The more we share together,
The happier we'll be.

For sharing is caring and caring is sharing,
The more we share together,
The happier we'll be.

Charlie over the Water

———— over the water,
———— over the sea,
———— catch a blackbird,
Can't catch me!

Open, Shut Them

Open, shut them; open, shut them;
Let your hands go clap, clap, clap.
Open, shut them; open, shut them;
Drop them in your lap, lap, lap.

Walk them, walk them, walk them, walk them,
Right up to your chin, chin, chin.
Open up your little mouth,
But do not let them in.

Book: _____

The Bear Went over the Mountain

The bear went over the mountain,
The bear went over the mountain,
The bear went over the mountain,
To see what he could see.

And all that he could see,
And all that he could see,
Was the other side of the mountain,
The other side of the mountain,
The other side of the mountain,
Was all that he could see.

Book: _____

Take Me Out to the Ballgame

Take me out to the ballgame,
Take me out to the park.
Buy me some peanuts and crackerjack,
I don't care if I never come back.
Let me root root root for the home team,
If they don't win it's a shame.
For it's one, two, three strikes "You're Out!"
At the old ballgame.

Down by the Station

Down by the station
Early in the morning.
See the little puffer bellies,
All in a row.
See the engine driver
Pull back on the throttle.
Chug, chug, toot, toot,
Off we go.

To Market, To Market

To market, to market, to buy a fat pig,
Home again, home again, jiggity jig.

To market, to market, to buy a fat hog,
Home again, home again, jiggity jog.

To market, to market, to buy some great toys,
Home again, home again, jiggity joys.

To market, to market, to buy some pork buns,
Home again, home again, market is done.

If You're Happy and You Know It

If you're happy and you know it,
  clap your hands.
If you're happy and you know it,
  clap your hands.
If you're happy and you know it,
And you really want to show it,
If you're happy and you know it,
  clap your hands.

Stamp your feet! Shout hooray! Do all three!

23 Cat and Mouse

Suggested Books

Kemp, *Hickory, Dickory, Dock*
Kraus, *Where Are You Going, Little Mouse?*
———, *Whose Mouse Are You?*
Any books listed for the "Cats and Kittens" program.

Opening Song

The More We Get Together

The music is in *Eye Winker, Tom Tinker . . .* and *The Raffi Singable Songbook.* This song can just be sung or you can add the finger-game aspects.

Verse 1: Hug yourself and sway side to side. Point both fingers to "your friends," then touch yourself on "my friends," then back to hugging.

Verse 2: Clasp hands and sway back and forth. Shake hands with person nearest you, or all hold hands.

Name Song and Finger Game

Charlie over the Water

The music is in *Eye Winker, Tom Tinker . . . .*

Point to everyone for the first two lines. Clap hands on "blackbird," then point to yourself for last line.

Opening Finger Game

Open, Shut Them

Suit actions to words.

Finger Game

Hickory, Dickory, Dock

Place elbow of one arm in the palm of the other hand;
Swing arm back and forth three times;
Run hand up child's arm;
Hold up one finger;
Run hand down child's arm;
Swing arm again.

Verse 2: Hold up two fingers;
Place hands around mouth and say "Boo!"

Verse 3: Hold up three fingers;
Hold arms out wide and say "Wee!"

Song

Pussy Cat, Pussy Cat

The music is in *The Fireside Song Book of Birds and Beasts, The Baby's Song Book,* and *Singing Bee!*

Song

Three Little Kittens

The music is in *The Baby's Song Book* and *Singing Bee!*

Tickle

Here Comes a Mouse

Touch child's foot;
Run hand up leg;
Run hand up under arm and tickle.

Closing Song

If You're Happy and You Know It

This well-known song and finger game can be found in *Do Your Ears Hang Low?* or *Ring a Ring o' Roses.* Suit actions to words, clapping and stamping twice, shouting "hooray" once, and repeating them all for "Do all three!"

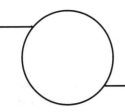

Cat and Mouse

The More We Get Together

The more we get together, together, together,
The more we get together,
The happier we'll be.

For your friends are my friends
And my friends are your friends.
The more we get together,
The happier we'll be.

The more we share together,
Together, together,
The more we share together,
The happier we'll be.

For sharing is caring and caring is sharing,
The more we share together,
The happier we'll be.

Charlie over the Water

———— over the water,
———— over the sea,
———— catch a blackbird,
Can't catch me!

Open, Shut Them

Open, shut them; open, shut them;
Let your hands go clap, clap, clap.
Open, shut them; open, shut them;
Drop them in your lap, lap, lap.

Walk them, walk them, walk them, walk them,
Right up to your chin, chin, chin.
Open up your little mouth,
But do not let them in.

Book: _____

Hickory, Dickory, Dock

Hickory, dickory, dock
The mouse ran up the clock
The clock struck one
The mouse ran down
Hickory, dickory, dock.

. . . The clock struck two
The mouse said Boo!

. . . The clock struck three
The mouse said Weeee!

Pussy Cat, Pussy Cat

Pussy cat, pussy cat, where have you been?
I've been to London to visit the queen.
Pussy cat, pussy cat, what did you there?
I frightened the little mouse under her chair.

Book: _____

Three Little Kittens

Three little kitten, they lost their mittens,
And they began to cry.
Oh, Mother dear, see here, see here,
Our mittens we have lost.
What lost your mittens! You naughty kittens!
Then you shall have no pie.
Meow, meow, meow, meow!

Three little kittens, they found their mittens,
And they began to cry,
Oh Mother dear, see hear, see here,
Our mittens we have found.
What found your mittens, you darling kittens,
Then you shall have some pie.
Purr, purr, purr, purr!

Here Comes a Mouse

Here comes a mouse,
Squeak, squeak, squeak,
He is tiny and soft
And has pink little feet.

He runs up your leg,
Then under your arm,
Ticklety, ticklety,
But he means you no harm.

If You're Happy and You Know It

If you're happy and you know it,
 clap your hands.
If you're happy and you know it,
 clap your hands.
If you're happy and you know it,
And you really want to show it,
If you're happy and you know it,
 clap your hands.

Stamp your feet! Shout hooray! Do all three!

24 Cats and Kittens

Suggested Books

Brown, *Our Cat Flossie*
Cauley, *Three Little Kittens*
Ehlert, *Feathers for Lunch*
Halpern, *Little Robin Redbreast*
McMillan, *Kitten Can*

Opening Song

The More We Get Together

The music is in *Eye Winker, Tom Tinker* . . . and *The Raffi Singable Songbook.* This song can just be sung or you can add the finger-game aspects.

Verse 1: Hug yourself and sway side to side. Point both fingers to "your friends," then touch yourself on "my friends," then back to hugging.

Verse 2: Clasp hands and sway back and forth. Shake hands with person nearest you, or all hold hands.

Name Song and Finger Game

Charlie over the Water

The music is in *Eye Winker, Tom Tinker* . . . .

Point to everyone for the first two lines. Clap hands on "blackbird," then point to yourself for last line.

Opening Finger Game

Open, Shut Them

Suit actions to words.

Song

Pussy Cat, Pussy Cat

The music is in *The Fireside Song Book of Birds and Beasts, The Baby's Song Book,* and *Singing Bee!*

Song

Three Little Kittens

The music is in *The Baby's Song Book, The Fireside Song Book of Birds and Beasts,* and *Singing Bee!*

Tickle

The Bumblebee

Put forefinger and thumb together for the bee; Fly bee around and then tickle child anywhere.

Closing Song

If You're Happy and You Know It

This well-known song and finger game can be found in *Do Your Ears Hang Low?* or *Ring a Ring o' Roses.* Suit actions to words, clapping and stamping twice, shouting "hooray" once, and repeating them all for "Do all three!"

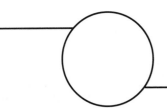

Cats and Kittens

The More We Get Together

The more we get together, together, together,
The more we get together,
The happier we'll be.

For your friends are my friends
And my friends are your friends.
The more we get together,
The happier we'll be.

The more we share together,
Together, together,
The more we share together,
The happier we'll be.

For sharing is caring and caring is sharing,
The more we share together,
The happier we'll be.

Charlie over the Water

———— over the water,
———— over the sea,
———— catch a blackbird,
Can't catch me!

Open, Shut Them

Open, shut them; open, shut them;
Let your hands go clap, clap, clap.
Open, shut them; open, shut them;
Drop them in your lap, lap, lap.

Walk them, walk them, walk them, walk them,
Right up to your chin, chin, chin.
Open up your little mouth,
But do not let them in.

Book: _____

Pussy Cat, Pussy Cat

Pussy cat, pussy cat,
where have you been?
I've been to London to
visit the Queen.
Pussy cat, pussy cat,
what did you there?
I frightened the little
mouse under her chair.

Book: _____

Three Little Kittens

Three little kittens, they lost their mittens,
And they began to cry.
Oh Mother dear, we sadly fear
Our mittens we have lost.
What lost your mittens, you naughty kittens.
Then you shall have no pie.
Meow, meow, meow, meow!

Three little kittens, they found their mittens,
And they began to cry,
Oh Mother dear, see here, see here.
Our mittens we have found.
What found your mittens, you darling kittens,
Then you shall have some pie.
Purr, purr, purr, purr!

Three little kittens put on their mittens
And soon ate up the pie.
Oh Mother dear, we greatly fear
Our mittens we have soiled.
What soiled your mittens, you naughty kittens,
Then they began to sigh.
Meow, meow, meow, meow!

Three little kittens washed their mittens,
And hung them up to dry.
Oh Mother dear, look here, look here,
Our mittens we have washed.
What washed your mittens, you darling kittens,
But hush! I smell a rat close by.
Meow, meow, meow, meow!

The Bumblebee

A bumblebee comes around the barn,
With a bundle of stingers under his arm.
Buzzzzzzz!

If You're Happy and You Know It

If you're happy and you know it,
  clap your hands.
If you're happy and you know it,
  clap your hands.
If you're happy and you know it,
And you really want to show it,
If you're happy and you know it,
  clap your hands.

Stamp your feet! Shout hooray! Do all three!

25 Going to the Dogs

Suggested Books

Burningham, *The Dog*
Harper, *My Dog Rosie*
Hawkins, *Old Mother Hubbard*
Hill (Almost any of the "Spot" books)
Oxenbury, *Tom and Pippo and the Dog*

Opening Song

The More We Get Together

The music is in *Eye Winker, Tom Tinker* . . . and *The Raffi Singable Songbook*. This song can just be sung or you can add the finger-game aspects.

Verse 1: Hug yourself and sway side to side. Point both fingers to "your friends," then touch yourself on "my friends," then back to hugging.

Verse 2: Clasp hands and sway back and forth. Shake hands with person nearest you, or all hold hands.

Name Song and Finger Game

Charlie over the Water

The music is in *Eye Winker, Tom Tinker* . . . .

Point to everyone for the first two lines. Clap hands on "blackbird," then point to yourself for last line.

Opening Finger Game

Open, Shut Them

Suit actions to words.

Song and Finger Game

Bingo

The music is in *Go In and Out the Window, Reader's Digest Children's Songbook* and *Singing Bee!*

Clap instead of singing the letter where indicated.

Song

Where, Oh Where Has My Little Dog Gone?

The music is in *Singing Bee!*

Song

My Puppy Lies over the Ocean

Sung to the tune "My Bonnie Lies over the Ocean." The music is in *Go In and Out the Window*.

Sway back and forth while singing this silly adaptation.

Song and Finger Game

Paws, Muzzles, Ears and Tails

Sung to the tune "Head, Shoulders, Knees and Toes." The music is in *Do Your Ears Hang Low?*

Curl hands in front for paws;
Touch nose, ears, and rears for muzzle, ears, and tail;
Tickle child all over for "Fur and fleas," etc.;
Repeat a second time, but faster.

Closing Song

If You're Happy and You Know It

This well-known song and finger game can be found in *Do Your Ears Hang Low?* or *Ring a Ring o' Roses*. Suit actions to words, clapping and stamping twice, shouting "hooray" once, and repeating them all for "Do all three!"

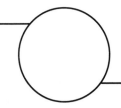

Going to the Dogs

The More We Get Together

The more we get together, together, together,
The more we get together,
The happier we'll be.

For your friends are my friends
And my friends are your friends.
The more we get together,
The happier we'll be.

The more we share together,
Together, together,
The more we share together,
The happier we'll be.

For sharing is caring and caring is sharing,
The more we share together,
The happier we'll be.

Charlie over the Water

——— over the water,
——— over the sea,
——— catch a blackbird,
Can't catch me!

Open, Shut Them

Open, shut them; open, shut them;
Let your hands go clap, clap, clap.
Open, shut them; open, shut them;
Drop them in your lap, lap, lap.

Walk them, walk them, walk them, walk them,
Right up to your chin, chin, chin.
Open up your little mouth,
But do not let them in.

Book: _____

Bingo

There was a farmer had a dog,
And Bingo was his name-o.
B I N G O, B I N G O, B I N G O,
And Bingo was his name-o.

(clap) I N G O, . . .
(clap clap) N G O, . . .
(clap clap clap) G O, . . .
(clap clap clap clap) O, . . .
(clap clap clap clap clap), . . .
(Repeat first verse.)

Where, Oh Where Has My Little Dog Gone?

Where, oh where has my little dog gone?
Oh where, oh where can he be?
With his ears cut short
And his tail cut long.
Oh, where oh where
  can he be?

Book: _____

My Puppy Lies over the Ocean

My puppy lies over the ocean,
My puppy lies over the sea,
My puppy lies over the ocean,
Please bring back my puppy to me.

Refrain:·
Bring back, bring back,
Oh, bring back my puppy to me, to me.
Bring back, bring back,
Oh, bring back my puppy to me.

Oh, blow ye winds over the ocean,
And blow ye winds over the sea,
Oh, blow ye winds over the ocean,
And bring back my puppy to me.
(Repeat refrain.)

Paws, Muzzles, Ears and Tails

Paws, muzzles, ears and tails, ears and tails.
Paws, muzzles, ears and tails, ears and tails.
Fur and fleas and ticks and snails.
Paws, muzzles, ears and tails, ears and tails.

If You're Happy and You Know It

If you're happy and you know it,
  clap your hands.
If you're happy and you know it,
  clap your hands.
If you're happy and you know it,
And you really want to show it,
If you're happy and you know it,
  clap your hands.

Stamp your feet! Shout hooray! Do all three!

26 On the Farm

Suggested Books

Berry, *Old MacDonald Had a Farm*
Fleming, *Barnyard Banter*
Ginsburg, *Good Morning, Chick*
Hill, *Spot Goes to the Farm*
Hutchins, *Rosie's Walk*
Slobodkinia, *The Wonderful Feast*
Tafuri, *Spots, Feathers and Curly Tails*
———, *This Is the Farmer*
Williams, *I Went Walking*

Opening Song

The More We Get Together

The music is in *Eye Winker, Tom Tinker* . . . and *The Raffi Singable Songbook*. This song can just be sung or you can add the finger-game aspects.

Verse 1: Hug yourself and sway side to side. Point both fingers to "your friends," then touch yourself on "my friends," then back to hugging.

Verse 2: Clasp hands and sway back and forth. Shake hands with person nearest you, or all hold hands.

Name Song and Finger Game

Charlie over the Water

The music is in *Eye Winker, Tom Tinker* . . . .

Point to everyone for the first two lines. Clap hands on "blackbird," then point to yourself for last line.

Opening Finger Game

Open, Shut Them

Suit actions to words.

Song

Baa, Baa, Black Sheep

The music is in *The Baby's Song Book, Reader's Digest Children's Songbook, Go In and Out the Window* and *Singing Bee!*

Finger Game

Clap Your Hands

Suit action to words.

Song

The Farmer in the Dell

The music is in *Go In and Out the Window* and *Singing Bee!*

Lap Jog

Old Farmer Giles

Jog child on lap;
Lift child up on last line;
Others can clap along.

Closing Song

If You're Happy and You Know It

This well-known song and finger game can be found in *Do Your Ears Hang Low?* or *Ring a Ring o' Roses*. Suit actions to words, clapping and stamping twice, shouting "hooray" once, and repeating them all for "Do all three!"

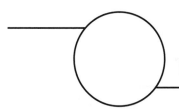

On the Farm

The More We Get Together

The more we get together, together, together,
The more we get together,
The happier we'll be.

For your friends are my friends
And my friends are your friends.
The more we get together,
The happier we'll be.

The more we share together,
Together, together,
The more we share together,
The happier we'll be.

For sharing is caring and caring is sharing,
The more we share together,
The happier we'll be.

Charlie over the Water

———— over the water,
———— over the sea,
———— catch a blackbird,
Can't catch me!

Open, Shut Them

Open, shut them; open, shut them;
Let your hands go clap, clap, clap.
Open, shut them; open, shut them;
Drop them in your lap, lap, lap.

Walk them, walk them, walk them, walk them,
Right up to your chin, chin, chin.
Open up your little mouth,
But do not let them in.

Book: _____

Baa, Baa, Black Sheep

Baa, baa, black sheep, have you any wool?
Yes sir, yes sir, three bags full.
One for my master and one for my dame,
And one for the little boy
Who lives down the lane.
Baa, baa, black sheep, have you any wool?
Yes sir, yes sir, three bags full.

Clap Your Hands

Clap your hands, clap your hands,
Clap them just like me.
Touch your shoulders, touch your shoulders,
Touch them just like me.
Tap your knees, tap your knees,
Tap them just like me.
Shake your head, shake your head,
Shake it just like me.
Clap your hands, clap your hands,
Now let them quiet be.

Book: _____

The Farmer in the Dell

The farmer in the dell,
The farmer in the dell,
Heigh-ho the derry-o,
The farmer in the dell.

The farmer takes a wife, . . .
The wife takes a child, . . .
The child takes a nurse, . . .
The nurse takes a dog, . . .
The dog takes a cat, . . .
The cat takes a rat, . . .
The rat takes the cheese, . . .
The CHEESE stands alone, . . .

Old Farmer Giles

Old farmer Giles
He went seven miles
With his faithful dog Rover;

And old farmer Giles
When he came to a stile
Took a run and JUMPED CLEAN OVER!

If You're Happy and You Know It

If you're happy and you know it,
    clap your hands.
If you're happy and you know it,
    clap your hands.
If you're happy and you know it,
And you really want to show it,
If you're happy and you know it,
    clap your hands.

Stamp your feet! Shout hooray! Do all three!

27 Chicks and Ducklings

Suggested Books

Ginsburg, *Across the Stream*
————, *Chick and the Duckling*
Raffi, *Five Little Ducks*
Tafuri, *Have You Seen My Duckling?*

Opening Song

The More We Get Together

The music is in *Eye Winker, Tom Tinker* . . . and *The Raffi Singable Songbook*. This song can just be sung or you can add the finger-game aspects.

Verse 1: Hug yourself and sway side to side. Point both fingers to "your friends," then touch yourself on "my friends," then back to hugging.

Verse 2: Clasp hands and sway back and forth. Shake hands with person nearest you, or all hold hands.

Name Song and Finger Game

Charlie over the Water

The music is in *Eye Winker, Tom Tinker* . . . .

Point to everyone for the first two lines. Clap hands on "blackbird," then point to yourself for last line.

Opening Finger Game

Open, Shut Them

Suit actions to words.

Song and Finger Game

Quacking Ducks

The music is in *Eye Winker, Tom Tinker* . . . under the title "Five Little Ducks."

Hold up five fingers;
Make fingers run away behind back;
Make quacking motion with thumb and four
    fingers;
Four fingers run back;
Repeat actions with appropriate number of
    fingers.

Song and Finger Game

Fun with Hands

Sung to the tune "Row, Row, Row Your Boat." The music is in *Singing Bee!*

Suit action to words.

Rhyme and Lap Jog

Cock Crows in the Morn

Jog child on lap;
Others can clap along.

Closing Song

If You're Happy and You Know It

This well-known song and finger game can be found in *Do Your Ears Hang Low?* or *Ring a Ring o' Roses*. Suit actions to words, clapping and stamping twice, shouting "hooray" once, and repeating them all for "Do all three!"

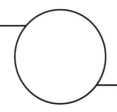

Chicks and Ducklings

The More We Get Together
The more we get together, together, together,
The more we get together,
The happier we'll be.

For your friends are my friends
And my friends are your friends.
The more we get together,
The happier we'll be.

The more we share together,
Together, together,
The more we share together,
The happier we'll be.

For sharing is caring and caring is sharing,
The more we share together,
The happier we'll be.

Charlie over the Water
———— over the water,
———— over the sea,
———— catch a blackbird,
Can't catch me!

Open, Shut Them
Open, shut them; open, shut them;
Let your hands go clap, clap, clap.
Open, shut them; open, shut them;
Drop them in your lap, lap, lap.

Walk them, walk them, walk them, walk them,
Right up to your chin, chin, chin.
Open up your little mouth,
But do not let them in.

Book: _____

Quacking Ducks
Five little ducks went out to play,
Over the hills and far away.
Mama Duck said, "Quack, Quack, Quack."
Four little ducks came running back.

Four little ducks went out to play, . . .
Three little ducks went out to play, . . .
Two little ducks went out to play, . . .

One little duck went out to play,
Over the hill and far away.
Mama Duck said, "Quack, Quack, Quack."
No little ducks came running back.

No little ducks went out to play,
Over the hill and far away.
Daddy Duck said, "Quack, Quack, Quack."
Five little ducks came running back.

Fun with Hands
Roll, roll, roll your hands
As slowly as can be,
Roll, roll, roll your hands;
Do it now with me.

Shake, shake, shake your hands, . . .
Fold, fold, fold your hands, . . .

Book: _____

Cock Crows in the Morn
Cock crows in the morn
To tell us to rise,
And he who lies late
Will never be wise;

For early to bed
And early to rise,
Is the way to be healthy
And wealthy and wise.

If You're Happy and You Know It
If you're happy and you know it,
  clap your hands.
If you're happy and you know it,
  clap your hands.
If you're happy and you know it,
And you really want to show it,
If you're happy and you know it,
  clap your hands.

Stamp your feet! Shout hooray! Do all three!

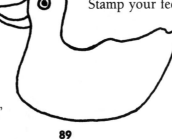

28 Bears, Oh My

Suggested Books

Arnosky, *Every Autumn Comes the Bear*
Dabcovich, *Sleepy Bear*
Gretz, *Teddy Bears 1 to 10*
Jonas, *Two Bear Cubs*
Maris, *Are You There, Bear?*

Opening Song

The More We Get Together

The music is in *Eye Winker, Tom Tinker . . .* and *The Raffi Singable Songbook*. This song can just be sung or you can add the finger-game aspects.

Verse 1: Hug yourself and sway side to side. Point both fingers to "your friends," then touch yourself on "my friends," then back to hugging.

Verse 2: Clasp hands and sway back and forth. Shake hands with person nearest you, or all hold hands.

Name Song and Finger Game

Charlie over the Water

The music is in *Eye Winker, Tom Tinker . . . .*

Point to everyone for the first two lines. Clap hands on "blackbird," then point to yourself for last line.

Opening Finger Game

Open, Shut Them

Suit actions to words.

Finger Game

Teddy Bear

Suit action to words.
Hug child or yourself for last line.

Song and Finger Game

This Is the Way We Wash Our Bears

Sung to the tune "The Mulberry Bush." The music is in *Go In and Out the Window* and *Singing Bee!*

Suit actions to words.

Song and Finger Game

The Bear Went over the Mountain

The music is in *Eye Winker, Tom Tinker . . .* and *Singing Bee!*

Climb hand up arm;
Shade eyes with hand and look around;
Climb hand down arm;
Look around again on last line.

Lap Jog

Boing! Boing! Squeak!

This poem by Jack Prelutsky can be found in his collection, *New Kid on the Block*. It also happens to make a great lap jog. This has been a favorite for years among infant-toddler programmers and their audiences. Enjoy.

Jog child on lap. Others can clap along.

Closing Song

If You're Happy and You Know It

This well-known song and finger game can be found in *Do Your Ears Hang Low?* or *Ring a Ring o' Roses*. Suit actions to words, clapping and stamping twice, shouting "hooray" once, and repeating them all for "Do all three!"

Bears, Oh My

The More We Get Together

The more we get together, together, together,
The more we get together,
The happier we'll be.

For your friends are my friends
And my friends are your friends.
The more we get together,
The happier we'll be.

The more we share together,
Together, together,
The more we share together,
The happier we'll be.

For sharing is caring and caring is
    sharing,
The more we share together,
The happier we'll be.

Charlie over the Water

———— over the water,
———— over the sea,
———— catch a blackbird,
Can't catch me!

Open, Shut Them

Open, shut them; open, shut them;
Let your hands go clap, clap, clap.
Open, shut them; open, shut them;
Drop them in your lap, lap, lap.

Walk them, walk them, walk them, walk them,
Right up to your chin, chin, chin.
Open up your little mouth,
But do not let them in.

Book: _____

Teddy Bear

Teddy bear, teddy bear, turn around;
Teddy bear, teddy bear, touch the ground.
Teddy bear, teddy bear, reach up high;
Teddy bear, teddy bear, touch the sky.
Teddy bear, teddy bear, touch your shoe;
Teddy bear, teddy bear, I love you.

This is the way we wash our bears,
Wash our bears, wash our bears.
This is the way we wash our bears,
So early in the morning.

. . . Dress our bears, . . .
. . . Feed our bears, . . .
. . . Hug our bears, . . .

Book: _____

The Bear Went over the Mountain

The bear went over the mountain,
The bear went over the mountain,
The bear went over the mountain,
To see what he could see.

And all that he could see,
And all that he could see,
Was the other side of the mountain,
The other side of the mountain,
The other side of the mountain,
Was all that he could see.

Boing! Boing! Squeak!

Refrain:
Boing! Boing! Squeak!
Boing! Boing! Squeak!
A bouncing mouse is in my house,
It's been here for a week.

It bounced from out of nowhere,
Then quickly settled in.
I'm grateful that it came alone—
(I've heard it has a twin),
It bounces in the kitchen,
It bounces in the den,
It bounces through the living room—
Look! There it goes again.
(Repeat refrain.)

If You're Happy and You Know It

If you're happy and you know it,
    clap your hands.
If you're happy and you know it,
    clap your hands.
If you're happy and you know it,
And you really want to show it,
If you're happy and you know it,
    clap your hands.

Stamp your feet! Shout hooray! Do all three!

29 Feathered Friends

Suggested Books

Ehlert, *Feathers for Lunch*
Halpern, *Little Robin Redbreast*
Hutchins, *Good-Night, Owl*
Janovitz, *Look Out, Bird*
Wolff, *A Year of Birds*

Opening Song

The More We Get Together

The music is in *Eye Winker, Tom Tinker* . . . and *The Raffi Singable Songbook.* This song can just be sung or you can add the finger-game aspects.

Verse 1: Hug yourself and sway side to side. Point both fingers to "your friends," then touch yourself on "my friends," then back to hugging.

Verse 2: Clasp hands and sway back and forth. Shake hands with person nearest you, or all hold hands.

Name Song and Finger Game

Charlie over the Water

The music is in *Eye Winker, Tom Tinker* . . . .

Point to everyone for the first two lines. Clap hands on "blackbird," then point to yourself for last line.

Opening Finger Game

Open, Shut Them

Suit actions to words.

Song

Little Robin Redbreast

Sung to the tune "Pop! Goes the Weasel." The music is in *Fireside Song Book of Birds and Beasts, Eye Winker, Tom Tinker* . . . , and *Singing Bee!*

Finger Game

Way Up High in the Apple Tree

Point up;
Make circles around eyes with thumbs and
    forefingers and look down;
Shake body;
Flutter fingers down to ground, pick up fruit,
    pretend to eat and rub stomach.

Any food can be used for this including pizza, etc.

Song

Sing a Song of Sixpence

The music is in *The Baby's Song Book, Reader's Digest Children's Songbook* and *Singing Bee!*

Rhyme and Lap Jog

Old Mother Goose

Jog child on lap;
Others can clap along.
Since this is so short, repeat twice if you wish.

Closing Song

If You're Happy and You Know It

This well-known song and finger game can be found in *Do Your Ears Hang Low?* or *Ring a Ring o' Roses.* Suit actions to words, clapping and stamping twice, shouting "hooray" once, and repeating them all for "Do all three!"

Feathered Friends

The More We Get Together

The more we get together, together, together,
The more we get together,
The happier we'll be.

For your friends are my friends
And my friends are your friends.
The more we get together,
The happier we'll be.

The more we share together,
Together, together,
The more we share together,
The happier we'll be.

For sharing is caring and caring is sharing,
The more we share together,
The happier we'll be.

Charlie over the Water

——— over the water,
——— over the sea,
——— catch a blackbird,
Can't catch me!

Open, Shut Them

Open, shut them; open, shut them;
Let your hands go clap, clap, clap.
Open, shut them; open, shut them;
Drop them in your lap, lap, lap.

Walk them, walk them, walk them, walk them,
Right up to your chin, chin, chin.
Open up your little mouth,
But do not let them in.

Book: _____

Little Robin Redbreast

Little Robin Redbreast
Sat upon a tree,
Up went Pussy-Cat,
Down went he.
Down came Pussy-Cat,
Away Robin ran,
Says Robin Redbreast:
"Catch me if you can!"

Little Robin Redbreast
Jumped upon a spade,
Pussy-Cat jumped after him,
And then he was afraid.
Little Robin chirped and sang,
And what did Pussy say?
Pussy said: "Mew, mew,"
And Robin flew away.

Book: _____

Way Up High in the Apple Tree

Way up high in the apple tree,
Two little eyes looking down at me.
So I shook that tree just as hard as I could,
Down came the apples, mmmm good!

Way up high in the banana tree, . . .
Way up high in the lollipop tree, . . .

Sing a Song of Sixpence

Sing a song of sixpence
A pocket full of rye;
Four-and-twenty blackbirds
Baked in a pie!

When the pie was opened
The birds began to sing;
Was not that a dainty dish
To set before the king?

Old Mother Goose

Old Mother Goose
When she wanted to wander
Would fly through the air
On a very fine gander.

If You're Happy and You Know It

If you're happy and you know it,
    clap your hands.
If you're happy and you know it,
    clap your hands.
If you're happy and you know it,
And you really want to show it,
If you're happy and you know it,
    clap your hands.

Stamp your feet! Shout hooray! Do all three!

30 Be Nice to Spiders

Suggested Book
    Carle, *Very Busy Spider*

Opening Song
    The More We Get Together

The music is in *Eye Winker, Tom Tinker . . .* and *The Raffi Singable Songbook*. This song can just be sung or you can add the finger-game aspects.

Verse 1: Hug yourself and sway side to side. Point both fingers to "your friends," then touch yourself on "my friends," then back to hugging.

Verse 2: Clasp hands and sway back and forth. Shake hands with person nearest you, or all hold hands.

Name Song and Finger Game
    Charlie over the Water

The music is in *Eye Winker, Tom Tinker . . . .*

Point to everyone for the first two lines. Clap hands on "blackbird," then point to yourself for last line.

Opening Finger Game
    Open, Shut Them

Suit actions to words.

Song and Finger Game
    Eentsy Weentsy Spider

The music is in *Eye Winker, Tom Tinker . . . .* There are several different versions of this fingergame. Here is one that works well with very young children.

One hand climbs up shoulder;
Raise hands high and slowly lower them;
Hand slides down arm;
Arms form circle over head;
Hand goes back up to shoulder.

Finger Game
    Fold Your Hands

Suit actions to words.

Rhyme
    Little Miss Muffet

Chant or rap and rhythmically clap.

Finger Game
    I'm Being Followed by a Big Brown Spider

This is a slightly different version of "I'm Being Swallowed by a Boa Constrictor," which can be found in *Ring a Ring o' Roses*.

Move a hand up the body along with the verses; For the last line, ruffle hair with hand.

Closing Song
    If You're Happy and You Know It

This well-known song and finger game can be found in *Do Your Ears Hang Low?* or *Ring a Ring o' Roses*. Suit actions to words, clapping and stamping twice, shouting "hooray" once, and repeating them all for "Do all three!"

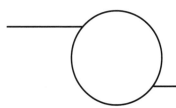

Be Nice to Spiders

The More We Get Together
The more we get together, together, together,
The more we get together,
The happier we'll be.

For your friends are my friends
And my friends are your friends.
The more we get together,
The happier we'll be.

The more we share together,
Together, together,
The more we share together,
The happier we'll be.

For sharing is caring and caring is sharing,
The more we share together,
The happier we'll be.

Charlie over the Water
———— over the water,
———— over the sea,
———— catch a blackbird,
Can't catch me!

Open, Shut Them
Open, shut them; open, shut them;
Let your hands go clap, clap, clap.
Open, shut them; open, shut them;
Drop them in your lap, lap, lap.

Walk them, walk them, walk them, walk them,
Right up to your chin, chin, chin.
Open up your little mouth,
But do not let them in.

Book: _____

Eentsy Weentsy Spider
The eentsy weentsy spider
Climbed up the water spout.
Down came the rain and
Washed the spider out.
Out came the sun and
dried up all the rain,
And the eentsy weentsy spider
Climbed up the spout again.

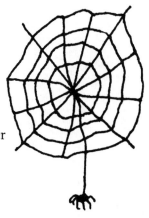

Fold Your Hands
Fold your hands so quietly.
Fold your hands like this you see.
Ready for a special look?
I'm going to read a special book.

Book: _____

Little Miss Muffet
Little Miss Muffet
Sat on a tuffet
Eating her curds and whey.
Along came a spider
And sat down beside her
And frightened Miss Muffet away.

I'm Being Followed by a Big Brown Spider
I'm being followed by a big brown spider,
I'm being followed by a big brown spider,
I'm being followed by a big brown spider,
And I don't like it very much.

Oh! No, no, no, she's up to my toe, toe, toe.
Oh! Gee, gee, gee, she's up to my knee, knee,
    knee.
Oh! Fiddle, fiddle, fiddle, she's up to my middle,
    middle, middle.
Oh! Heck, heck, heck, she's up to my neck,
    neck, neck.
Oh! Dread, dread, dread, she's on top of my
    head, head, head.
And she tickles, tickles, tickles.

If You're Happy and You Know It
If you're happy and you know it,
    clap your hands.
If you're happy and you know it,
    clap your hands.
If you're happy and you know it,
And you really want to show it,
If you're happy and you know it,
    clap your hands.

Stamp your feet! Shout hooray! Do all three!

31 Turtle Tales

Suggested Books

Asch, *Turtle Tale*
Florian, *Turtle Day*
Ormerod, *To Baby with Love* (the last story)

Opening Song

The More We Get Together

The music is in *Eye Winker, Tom Tinker . . .* and *The Raffi Singable Songbook*. This song can just be sung or you can add the finger-game aspects.

Verse 1: Hug yourself and sway side to side. Point both fingers to "your friends," then touch yourself on "my friends," then back to hugging.

Verse 2: Clasp hands and sway back and forth. Shake hands with person nearest you, or all hold hands.

Name Song and Finger Game

Charlie over the Water

The music is in *Eye Winker, Tom Tinker . . . .*

Point to everyone for the first two lines. Clap hands on "blackbird," then point to yourself for last line.

Opening Finger Game

Open, Shut Them

Suit actions to words.

Finger Game

Little Turtle

Hold out fist;
Cup hands to form box;
Swimming motions;
Climbing motion with hands;
Reach out and clap;
Repeat twice;
Turn hands toward self and snap;
Reach out and clap;
Repeat twice;
Point to self and shake head "No!"

Finger Game

This Is My Turtle

Make a fist;
Extend thumb;
Hide thumb in fist;
Extend thumb;
Hide thumb in fist.

Lap Jog

Boing! Boing! Squeak!

This poem by Jack Prelutsky can be found in his collection, *New Kid on the Block*. It also happens to make a great lap jog. This has been a favorite for years among infant-toddler programmers and their audiences. Enjoy.

Closing Song

If You're Happy and You Know It

This well-known song and finger game can be found in *Do Your Ears Hang Low?* or *Ring a Ring o' Roses*. Suit actions to words, clapping and stamping twice, shouting "hooray" once, and repeating them all for "Do all three!"

Turtle Tales

The More We Get Together

The more we get together, together, together,
The more we get together,
The happier we'll be.

For your friends are my friends
And my friends are your friends.
The more we get together,
The happier we'll be.

The more we share together,
Together, together,
The more we share together,
The happier we'll be.

For sharing is caring and caring is sharing,
The more we share together,
The happier we'll be.

Charlie over the Water

——— over the water,
——— over the sea,
——— catch a blackbird,
Can't catch me!

Open, Shut Them

Open, shut them; open, shut them;
Let your hands go clap, clap, clap.
Open, shut them; open, shut them;
Drop them in your lap, lap, lap.

Walk them, walk them, walk them, walk them,
Right up to your chin, chin, chin.
Open up your little mouth,
But do not let them in.

Book: _____

Little Turtle

There was a little turtle
And he lived in a box.
He swam in a puddle
And he climbed on a rock.

He snapped at the mosquito,
He snapped at the flea,
He snapped at the minnow,
And he snapped at me!

He caught the mosquito,
He caught the flea,
He caught the minnow,
But he didn't catch me!

Book: _____

This Is My Turtle

This is my turtle.
She lives in a shell.
She likes her home very well.
She pokes her head out
When she wants to eat.
And pulls it back in
When she wants to sleep.

Boing! Boing! Squeak!

Refrain:
Boing! Boing! Squeak!
Boing! Boing! Squeak!
A bouncing mouse is in my house,
It's been here for a week.

It bounced from out of nowhere
Then quickly settled in,
I'm grateful that it came alone
(I've heard it has a twin),
It bounces in the kitchen,
It bounces in the den,
It bounces through the living room—
Look! There it goes again.
(Repeat refrain.)

If You're Happy and You Know It

If you're happy and you know it,
    clap your hands.
If you're happy and you know it,
    clap your hands.
If you're happy and you know it,
And you really want to show it,
If you're happy and you know it,
    clap your hands.

Stamp your feet! Shout hooray! Do all three!

32) Dinosaur Days

Suggested Books

Barton, *Dinosaurs, Dinosaurs*
Blumenthal, *Count-a-Saurus*

Opening Song

The More We Get Together

The music is in *Eye Winker, Tom Tinker . . .* and *The Raffi Singable Songbook*. This song can just be sung or you can add the finger-game aspects.

Verse 1: Hug yourself and sway side to side. Point both fingers to "your friends," then touch yourself on "my friends," then back to hugging.

Verse 2: Clasp hands and sway back and forth. Shake hands with person nearest you, or all hold hands.

Name Song and Finger Game

Charlie over the Water

The music is in *Eye Winker, Tom Tinker . . . .*

Point to everyone for the first two lines. Clap hands on "blackbird," then point to yourself for last line.

Opening Finger Game

Open, Shut Them

Suit actions to words.

Finger Game

Five Big Dinosaurs

Hold up five fingers;
Walk fingers away;
Hold up four fingers;
Repeat third line;
Continue to decrease fingers and suit actions to words.
On fourth line decrease number until last verse.

Song

Once upon a Time

Sung to the tune "The Little White Duck." The music is in *Eye Winker, Tom Tinker . . .* and *Reader's Digest Children's Songbook*.

Stamp feet for "Thump!"
Clap hands like jaws for "Crunch!"
Hold arms out to side and move up and down for "Flap!"

Closing Song

If You're Happy and You Know It

This well-known song and finger game can be found in *Do Your Ears Hang Low?* or *Ring a Ring o' Roses*. Suit actions to words, clapping and stamping twice, shouting "hooray" once, and repeating them all for "Do all three!"

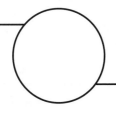

Dinosaur Days

The More We Get Together
The more we get together, together, together,
The more we get together,
The happier we'll be.

For your friends are my friends
And my friends are your friends.
The more we get together,
The happier we'll be.

The more we share together,
Together, together,
The more we share together,
The happier we'll be.

For sharing is caring and caring is sharing,
The more we share together,
The happier we'll be.

Charlie over the Water
———— over the water,
———— over the sea,
———— catch a blackbird,
Can't catch me!

Open, Shut Them
Open, shut them; open, shut them;
Let your hands go clap, clap, clap.
Open, shut them; open, shut them;
Drop them in your lap, lap, lap.

Walk them, walk them, walk them, walk them,
Right up to your chin, chin, chin.
Open up your little mouth,
But do not let them in.

Book: _____

Five Big Dinosaurs
Five big dinosaurs
Playing by the shore,
One went walking, and
Then there were four.

Four big dinosaurs,
Eating green seaweed,
One went walking, and
Then there were three.

Three big dinosaurs,
Finding plants to chew,
One went walking,
Then there were two.

Two big dinosaurs
Having so much fun,
One went walking,
Then there was one.

One lonely dinosaur
Decided not to roam,
She went walking, and
And walked right home.

Book: _____

Once upon a Time
Once upon a time long, long ago
There lived a dinosaur you all know.
The biggest dinosaur that ever was
Named Brachiosaurus and that's because
He was the biggest dinosaur that ever was.
Thump, Thump, Thump!

Once upon a time in the dark past
There lived a dinosaur; moved pretty fast.
The meanest dinosaur that there ever was
Tyrannosaur Rex was his name because
He was the meanest dinosaur that ever was.
Crunch, Crunch, Crunch!

Once upon a time in the olden days,
There lived a dinosaur that had strange ways.
The flyingest dinosaur that ever was
Named Pterodactyl and that's because
He was the flyingest dinosaur that ever was.
Flap, Flap, Flap!

If You're Happy and You Know It
If you're happy and you know it,
   clap your hands.
If you're happy and you know it,
   clap your hands.
If you're happy and you know it,
And you really want to show it,
If you're happy and you know it,
   clap your hands.

Stamp your feet! Shout hooray! Do all three!

99

33 Wildlife

Suggested Books

Arnosky, *Deer at the Brook*
Fleming, *In the Small Small Pond*
————, *In the Tall Tall Grass*
Gretz, *Hattie and the Fox*
Jorgensen, *Crocodile Beat*
Shaw, *Sheep Take a Hike*
Wallwork, *No Dodos*
Wolff, *A Year of Beasts*
Any books listed for the "Bears," "Feathered Friends," or "Turtle Tales" programs.

Opening Song

The More We Get Together

The music is in *Eye Winker, Tom Tinker . . .* and *The Raffi Singable Songbook*. This song can just be sung or you can add the finger-game aspects.

Verse 1: Hug yourself and sway side to side. Point both fingers to "your friends," then touch yourself on "my friends," then back to hugging.

Verse 2: Clasp hands and sway back and forth. Shake hands with person nearest you, or all hold hands.

Name Song and Finger Game

Charlie over the Water

The music is in *Eye Winker, Tom Tinker . . . .*

Point to everyone for the first two lines. Clap hands on "blackbird," then point to yourself for last line.

Opening Finger Game

Open, Shut Them

Suit actions to words.

Song

Home on the Range

The music is in *Go In and Out the Window* and *Songs America Sings*.

Finger Game

Fold Your Hands

Fold hands in front of you;
Lay them in lap;
Pick up book and show it.

Song

Animals Are Hard To See

Sung to the tune "Little Brown Jug."

Tickle

There Came a Little Mouse

Try this tickle from Norway.

Creep two fingers up child's arm;
At "but there!" tickle under the chin.

Closing Song

If You're Happy and You Know It

This well-known song and finger game can be found in *Do Your Ears Hang Low?* or *Ring a Ring o' Roses*. Suit actions to words, clapping and stamping twice, shouting "hooray" once, and repeating them all for "Do all three!"

Wildlife

The More We Get Together

The more we get together, together, together,
The more we get together,
The happier we'll be.

For your friends are my friends
And my friends are your friends.
The more we get together,
The happier we'll be.

The more we share together,
Together, together,
The more we share together,
The happier we'll be.

For sharing is caring and caring is sharing,
The more we share together,
The happier we'll be.

Charlie over the Water

———— over the water,
———— over the sea,
———— catch a blackbird,
Can't catch me!

Open, Shut Them

Open, shut them; open, shut them;
Let your hands go clap, clap, clap.
Open, shut them; open, shut them;
Drop them in your lap, lap, lap.

Walk them, walk them, walk them, walk them,
Right up to your chin, chin, chin.
Open up your little mouth,
But do not let them in.

Book: _____

Home on the Range

Oh, give me a home where the buffalo roam,
Where the deer and the antelope play,
Where seldom is heard a discouraging word,
And the skies are not cloudy all day.

Home, home on the range,
Where the deer and the antelope play.
Where seldom is heard a discouraging word,
And the skies are not cloudy all day.

Fold Your Hands

Fold your hands so quietly,
Fold your hands like this you see.
Ready for a special look?
I'm going to read a special book.

Book: _____

Animals Are Hard To See

Animals are hard to see
In the jungle filled with trees
But be careful, look just right
You might see a parrot bright.

> _Refrain:_
> Ho, ho, ho, you and me,
> See the animals in the trees
> Ho, ho, ho, you and me,
> See the animals in the trees.

Went to view some monkeys fine
A'swinging from vine to vine
We were quiet as could be
They were so much fun to see.
(Repeat refrain.)

Heard a roar and looked around
Wondered what could make that sound
There were tigers looking back
Thinking we would make a snack.

Ho, ho, ho, you and me
See the people in the trees
Ho, ho, ho, you and me
Yummy people if you please.

There Came a Little Mouse

There came a little mouse,
Who would like to find a house.
Not here, but there!

If You're Happy and You Know It

If you're happy and you know it,
  clap your hands.
If you're happy and you know it,
  clap your hands.
If you're happy and you know it,
And you really want to show it,
If you're happy and you know it,
  clap your hands.

Stamp your feet! Shout hooray! Do all three!

101

34 Happy New Year

Suggested Books

Florian, *A Winter Day*
————, *A Year in the Country*
Wolff, *A Year of Beasts*
————, *A Year of Birds*

Opening Song

The More We Get Together

The music is in *Eye Winker, Tom Tinker . . .* and *The Raffi Singable Songbook*. This song can just be sung or you can add the finger-game aspects.

Verse 1: Hug yourself and sway side to side. Point both fingers to "your friends," then touch yourself on "my friends," then back to hugging.

Verse 2: Clasp hands and sway back and forth. Shake hands with person nearest you, or all hold hands.

Name Song and Finger Game

Charlie over the Water

The music is in *Eye Winker, Tom Tinker . . . .*

Point to everyone for the first two lines. Clap hands on "blackbird," then point to yourself for last line.

Opening Finger Game

Open, Shut Them

Suit actions to words.

Finger Game

Hickory, Dickory, Dock

Place elbow of one arm in the palm of the other hand;
Swing arm back and forth three times;
Run hand up child's arm;
Hold up one finger;
Run hand down child's arm;
Swing arm again.

Verse 2: Hold up two fingers;
Place hands around mouth and say "Boo!"

Verse 3: Hold up three fingers;
Hold arms out wide and say "Wee!"

Song

Auld Lang Syne

The music is in *Songs America Sings*. This traditional New Year song started in the late 1700s when Scottish poet Robert Burns copied down the song from an old man and added several verses.

Lap Jog

Bounce Me

Jog child on lap. Others can clap along.

Closing Song

If You're Happy and You Know It

This well-known song and finger game can be found in *Do Your Ears Hang Low?* or *Ring a Ring o' Roses*. Suit actions to words, clapping and stamping twice, shouting "hooray" once, and repeating them all for "Do all three!"

Happy New Year

The More We Get Together

The more we get together, together, together,
The more we get together,
The happier we'll be.

For your friends are my friends
And my friends are your friends.
The more we get together,
The happier we'll be.

The more we share together,
Together, together,
The more we share together,
The happier we'll be.

For sharing is caring and caring is sharing,
The more we share together,
The happier we'll be.

Charlie over the Water

——— over the water,
——— over the sea,
——— catch a blackbird,
Can't catch me!

Open, Shut Them

Open, shut them; open, shut them;
Let your hands go clap, clap, clap.
Open, shut them; open, shut them;
Drop them in your lap, lap, lap.

Walk them, walk them, walk them, walk them,
Right up to your chin, chin, chin.
Open up your little mouth,
But do not let them in.

Book: _____

Hickory, Dickory, Dock

Hickory, dickory, dock,
The mouse ran up the clock,
The clock struck one and
The mouse ran down,
Hickory, dickory, dock.

. . . The clock struck two,
And the mouse said Boo!

. . . The clock struck three,
And the mouse said Weeee!

Book: _____

Auld Lang Syne

Should auld acquaintance be forgot,
And never brought to mind?
Should auld acquaintance be forgot,
And days of auld lang syne?

Refrain:
For auld lang syne, my dear,
For auld lang syne,
We'll take a cup o' kindness yet,
For auld lang syne.

Bounce Me

Bounce me, bounce me,
On your knee.
Bounce me, bounce me,
Pretty please.
Bounce me, bounce me,
Here and there.
Bounce me, bounce me,
Everywhere.

If You're Happy and You Know It

If you're happy and you know it,
   clap your hands.
If you're happy and you know it,
   clap your hands.
If you're happy and you know it,
And you really want to show it,
If you're happy and you know it,
   clap your hands.

Stamp your feet! Shout hooray! Do all three!

35 Chinese New Year / Chinese Zodiac Animals

Suggested Books

Hale, *Mary Had a Little Lamb*
Ill. by DePaola
———, *Mary Had a Little Lamb*
Photos by McMillan
Kemp, *Baa, Baa, Black Sheep*
Tafuri, *Spots, Feathers and Curly Tails*
Any of the books listed for the "Going to the Dogs" program or any book with a Chinese zodiac animal in it.

Opening Song

The More We Get Together

The music is in *Eye Winker, Tom Tinker . . .* and *The Raffi Singable Songbook*. This song can just be sung or you can add the finger-game aspects.

Verse 1: Hug yourself and sway side to side. Point both fingers to "your friends," then touch yourself on "my friends," then back to hugging.

Verse 2: Clasp hands and sway back and forth. Shake hands with person nearest you, or all hold hands.

Name Song and Finger Game

Charlie over the Water

The music is in *Eye Winker, Tom Tinker . . . .*

Point to everyone for the first two lines. Clap hands on "blackbird," then point to yourself for last line.

Opening Finger Game

Open, Shut Them

Suit actions to words.

Poem or Song

Chinese Lion Dancers

Chant or rap while clapping rhythmically. This can also be sung to the tune "I'm a Little Teapot." The music is in *Music for Ones and Twos* and *Singing Bee!*

Finger Game

Firecrackers

Have everyone quietly begin to clap erratically; Clap louder and louder; Now begin to clap softly again and stop.

Song

Old MacDonald Had a Farm

The music is in *Go In and Out the Window, Reader's Digest Children's Songbook* and *Singing Bee!*

This version uses all of the twelve zodiac animals in their correct order starting with the "Year of the Rat." Because there are so many animals it is recommended that the cumulative version not be used. Gung Hay Fat Choy!

Lap Jog

To Market, To Market

Jog child on lap. Others can clap along.

Closing Song

If You're Happy and You Know It

This well-known song and finger game can be found in *Do Your Ears Hang Low?* or *Ring a Ring o' Roses*. Suit actions to words, clapping and stamping twice, shouting "hooray" once, and repeating them all for "Do all three!"

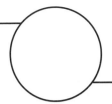

Chinese New Year /
Chinese Zodiac Animals

The More We Get Together
The more we get together, together, together,
The more we get together,
The happier we'll be.

For your friends are my friends
And my friends are your friends.
The more we get together,
The happier we'll be.

The more we share together,
Together, together,
The more we share together,
The happier we'll be.

For sharing is caring and caring is sharing,
The more we share together,
The happier we'll be.

Charlie over the Water
——— over the water,
——— over the sea,
——— catch a blackbird,
Can't catch me!

Open, Shut Them
Open, shut them; open, shut them;
Let your hands go clap, clap, clap.
Open, shut them; open, shut them;
Drop them in your lap, lap, lap.

Walk them, walk them, walk them, walk them,
Right up to your chin, chin, chin.
Open up your little mouth,
But do not let them in.

Book: _____

Chinese Lion Dancers
Chinese lion dancers
Leap down the street.
Throwing lots of candy
That is good to eat.
Loud firecrackers
Cheer everyone.
The New Year's parade
Has just begun.

Firecrackers

Book: _____

Old McDonald Had a Farm
Old MacDonald had a farm, E I E I O.
And on this farm he had a Rat, E I E I O.
With a squeak squeak here,
And a squeak squeak there,
Here a squeak, there a squeak,
Everywhere a squeak,
Old MacDonald had a farm, E I E I O!

Ox - Snort!
Tiger - Growl!
Rabbit - Hop!
Dragon - Roar!
Snake - Hiss!
Horse - Nay!
Sheep - Baa!
Monkey - Scratch!
Rooster - Cock-a-doodle!
Dog - Bark!
Pig - Oink!

To Market, To Market
To market, to market, to buy a fat pig,
Home again, home again, jiggity jig!

To market, to market, to buy a fat hog,
Home again, home again, jiggity jog!

If You're Happy and You Know It
If you're happy and you know it,
    clap your hands.
If you're happy and you know it,
    clap your hands.
If you're happy and you know it,
And you really want to show it,
If you're happy and you know it,
    clap your hands.

Stamp your feet! Shout hooray! Do all three!

36 Valentine's Day

Suggested Books

Kraus, *Whose Mouse Are You?*
Lear, *The Owl and the Pussycat*
Ill. by Brett

Opening Song

The More We Get Together

The music is in *Eye Winker, Tom Tinker . . .* and *The Raffi Singable Songbook*. This song can just be sung or you can add the finger-game aspects.

Verse 1: Hug yourself and sway side to side. Point both fingers to "your friends," then touch yourself on "my friends," then back to hugging.

Verse 2: Clasp hands and sway back and forth. Shake hands with person nearest you, or all hold hands.

Name Song and Finger Game

Charlie over the Water

The music is in *Eye Winker, Tom Tinker . . . .*

Point to everyone for the first two lines. Clap hands on "blackbird," then point to yourself for last line.

Opening Finger Game

Open, Shut Them

Suit actions to words.

Finger Game

Five Happy Valentines

Hold up five fingers and bend them down one at a time as verse progresses.

Song

The Riddle Song

The Music is in *Go In and Out the Window* and *Songs America Sings*. It is an eighteenth-century American courting song popularized by the mountain people of Kentucky. By posing a riddle, the woman gained time, and by solving the riddle her suitor was assured of her affection.

Finger Game

One I Love

Hold up ten fingers;
Touch them one by one as verse indicates;
At "Three I love you so!" hug child or self;
Hold up fingers again;
"Rock you to and fro!" rock child back and
   forth or rock arms;
Hold up fingers again:
"Eight, you love me too!" hug child or self;
Hold up fingers again:
"My bouncing Buckaroo!" jog child on lap while
   others clap along.

Closing Song

If You're Happy and You Know It

This well-known song and finger game can be found in *Do Your Ears Hang Low?* or *Ring a Ring o' Roses*. Suit actions to words, clapping and stamping twice, shouting "hooray" once, and repeating them all for "Do all three!"

Other Suggestions

Try the song "On the Good Ship Lollipop," found in the *Reader's Digest Children's Songbook*, or a favorite love song.

Valentine's Day

The More We Get Together
The more we get together, together, together,
The more we get together,
The happier we'll be.

For your friends are my friends
And my friends are your friends.
The more we get together,
The happier we'll be.

The more we share together,
Together, together,
The more we share together,
The happier we'll be.

For sharing is caring and caring is sharing,
The more we share together,
The happier we'll be.

Charlie over the Water
———— over the water,
———— over the sea,
———— catch a blackbird,
Can't catch me!

Open, Shut Them
Open, shut them; open, shut them;
Let your hands go clap, clap, clap.
Open, shut them; open, shut them;
Drop them in your lap, lap, lap.

Walk them, walk them, walk them, walk them,
Right up to your chin, chin, chin.
Open up your little mouth,
But do not let them in.

Book: _____

Five Happy Valentines
Five happy valentines from the ten-cent store,
I sent one to Mother, now there are four.
Four happy valentines, pretty ones to see,
I gave one to Brother, now there are three.
Three happy valentines, yellow, red, and blue,
I gave one to Sister, now there are two.
Two happy valentines, oh I'm having fun,
I gave one to Daddy, now there is one.
One happy valentine, the story's almost done,
I gave it to Baby, and now there are none.

Book: _____

The Riddle Song
I gave my love a cherry that had no stone.
I gave my love a chicken that had no bone.
I gave my love a story that had no end.
I gave my love a baby that's no cryin'.

How can there be a cherry that has no stone?
How can there be a chicken that has no bone?
How can there be a story that has no end?
How can there be a baby that's no cryin'?

A cherry when it's blooming, it has no stone.
A chicken when it's pippin', it has no bone.
The story that I love you, it has no end.
A baby when it's sleeping, it's no cryin'.

One I Love
One I love you,
Two I love you,
Three I love you so!
Four I love you,
Five I love you,
Rock you to and fro!
Six I love you,
Seven I love you,
Eight, you love me too!
Nine I love you,
Ten I love you,
My bouncing buckaroo!

If You're Happy and You Know It
If you're happy and you know it,
 clap your hands.
If you're happy and you know it,
 clap your hands.
If you're happy and you know it,
And you really want to show it,
If you're happy and you know it,
 clap your hands.

Stamp your feet! Shout hooray! Do all three!

37 Wearing of the Green / St. Patrick's Day

Suggested Books

Any books listed for the "Color My World" program.

Opening Song

The More We Get Together

The music is in *Eye Winker, Tom Tinker* . . . and *The Raffi Singable Songbook*. This song can just be sung or you can add the finger-game aspects.

Verse 1: Hug yourself and sway side to side. Point both fingers to "your friends," then touch yourself on "my friends," then back to hugging.

Verse 2: Clasp hands and sway back and forth. Shake hands with person nearest you, or all hold hands.

Name Song and Finger Game

Charlie over the Water

The music is in *Eye Winker, Tom Tinker* . . . .

Point to everyone for the first two lines. Clap hands on "blackbird," then point to yourself for last line.

Opening Finger Game

Open, Shut Them

Suit actions to words.

Song

Molly Malone

The music is in *Reader's Digest Children's Songbook*.

Song

A Leprechaun No More

Sung to the tune "Down by the Riverside." The music is in *Go In and Out the Window* and under the title "Study War No More" in *I'm Going to Sing*.

Lap Jog

Leg over Leg

Jog child on lap while others clap along; Lift child up on last line.

Closing Song

If You're Happy and You Know It

This well-known song and finger game can be found in *Do Your Ears Hang Low?* or *Ring a Ring o' Roses*. Suit actions to words, clapping and stamping twice, shouting "hooray" once, and repeating them all for "Do all three!"

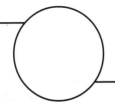

Wearing of the Green /
St. Patrick's Day

The More We Get Together

The more we get together, together, together,
The more we get together,
The happier we'll be.

For your friends are my friends
And my friends are your friends.
The more we get together,
The happier we'll be.

The more we share together,
Together, together,
The more we share together,
The happier we'll be.

For sharing is caring and caring is sharing,
The more we share together,
The happier we'll be.

Charlie over the Water

———— over the water,
———— over the sea,
———— catch a blackbird,
Can't catch me!

Open, Shut Them

Open, shut them; open, shut them;
Let your hands go clap, clap, clap.
Open, shut them; open, shut them;
Drop them in your lap, lap, lap.

Walk them, walk them, walk them, walk them,
Right up to your chin, chin, chin.
Open up your little mouth,
But do not let them in.

Book: _____

Molly Malone

In Dublin's fair city
Where the girls are so pretty,
'Twas there that I first met
Sweet Molly Malone;
She drove a wheelbarrow
Thro' streets broad and narrow,
Crying, "Cockles and mussels
Alive, alive-o!"

Refrain:
"Alive, alive-o! Alive, alive-o!"
Crying, "Cockles and mussels
Alive, alive-o!"

She was a fish monger
And sure 'twas no wonder,
Her father and mother
Were fish mongers too;
They drove wheelbarrows
Thro' streets broad and narrow,
Crying, "Cockles and mussels,
Alive, alive-o!"
(Repeat refrain.)

Book: _____

A Leprechaun No More

Gonna lay down my pot of gold,
Down by the riverside, down by the riverside,
Down by the riverside,
Gonna lay down my pot of gold,
Down by the riverside,
And not be a leprechaun no more.

I'm not gonna be a leprechaun,
I'm not gonna be a leprechaun,
I'm not gonna be a leprechaun no more.

I'm not gonna be a leprechaun,
I'm not gonna be a leprechaun,
I'm not gonna be a leprechaun no more.

Leg over Leg

Leg over leg,
As the dog went to Dover,
He came to a stile,
And JUMP, he went over.

If You're Happy and You Know It

If you're happy and you know it,
    clap your hands.
If you're happy and you know it,
    clap your hands.
If you're happy and you know it,
And you really want to show it,
If you're happy and you know it,
    clap your hands.

Stamp your feet! Shout hooray! Do all three!

38) Spring and Easter

Suggested Books

DePaola, *My First Easter*
Hill, *Spot's First Easter*
Tafuri, *Rabbit's Morning*
Wells, *Max's Chocolate Chicken*

Opening Song

The More We Get Together

The music is in *Eye Winker, Tom Tinker . . .* and *The Raffi Singable Songbook.* This song can just be sung or you can add the finger-game aspects.

Verse 1: Hug yourself and sway side to side. Point both fingers to "your friends," then touch yourself on "my friends," then back to hugging.

Verse 2: Clasp hands and sway back and forth. Shake hands with person nearest you, or all hold hands.

Name Song and Finger Game

Charlie over the Water

The music is in *Eye Winker, Tom Tinker . . . .*

Point to everyone for the first two lines. Clap hands on "blackbird," then point to yourself for last line.

Opening Finger Game

Open, Shut Them

Suit actions to words.

Song and Finger Game

My Ears Are Starting to Wiggle

Sung to the tune "The Bear Went over the Mountain." The music is in *Eye Winker, Tom Tinker . . . , Fireside Song Book of Birds and Beasts,* and *Singing Bee!*

Place hands on top of head like rabbit ears and wiggle them;
Place finger on nose and wiggle;
Put hands in front, curve and wiggle;
If standing up, shake rear end, otherwise move in chair.

Finger Game

Fold Your Hands

Fold hands in front of you;
Lay them in lap;
Pick up book and show it.

Song

I Saw Three Ships on Easter Day

Sung to the tune "I Saw Three Ships." The music is in *Singing Bee!*

Lap Jog

This Is the Way the Ladies Ride

Jog child on lap;
Lift child up on last line;
Others can clap along.

Closing Song

If You're Happy and You Know It

This well-known song and finger game can be found in *Do Your Ears Hang Low?* or *Ring a Ring o' Roses.* Suit actions to words, clapping and stamping twice, shouting "hooray" once, and repeating them all for "Do all three!"

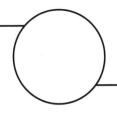

Spring and Easter

The More We Get Together
The more we get together, together, together,
The more we get together,
The happier we'll be.

For your friends are my friends
And my friends are your friends.
The more we get together,
The happier we'll be.

The more we share together,
Together, together,
The more we share together,
The happier we'll be.

For sharing is caring and caring is sharing,
The more we share together,
The happier we'll be.

Charlie over the Water
—— over the water,
—— over the sea,
—— catch a blackbird,
Can't catch me!

Open, Shut Them
Open, shut them; open, shut them;
Let your hands go clap, clap, clap.
Open, shut them; open, shut them;
Drop them in your lap, lap, lap.

Walk them, walk them, walk them, walk them,
Right up to your chin, chin, chin.
Open up your little mouth,
But do not let them in.

Book: _____

My Ears Are Starting to Wiggle
My ears are starting to wiggle,
My ears are starting to wiggle,
My ears are starting to wiggle,
Round and round
   and round.

My nose is starting
   to wiggle, . . .
My paws are starting
   to wiggle, . . .
My tail is starting
   to wiggle, . . .

Fold Your Hands
Fold your hands so quietly,
Fold your hands like this you see.
Ready for a special look?
I'm going to read a special book.

Book: _____

I Saw Three Ships on Easter Day
I saw three ships come sailing by,
A-sailing by, a-sailing by;
I saw three ships come sailing by,
On Easter day in the morning.

And what do you think was in them then,
Was in them then, was in them then?
And what do you think was in them then,
On Easter day in the morning?

Easter bunnies with baskets of eggs,
Baskets of eggs, baskets of eggs.
Easter bunnies with baskets of eggs,
On Easter day in the morning.

This Is the Way the Ladies Ride
This is the way the ladies ride,
Trit trit trot, trit trit trot.
This is the way the ladies ride,
Trit trit trot, trit trit trot!

This is the way the gentlemen ride,
Gallop-a-trot, gallop-a-trot.
This is the way the gentlemen ride,
Gallop-a-trot, gallop-a-trot!

And this is the way the babies ride,
Hobbledy-hoy, hobbledy-hoy,
This is the way the babies ride,
Hobbledy-hoy, hobbledy-hoy,
Hobbledy-hoy OVER the fence!

If You're Happy and You Know It
If you're happy and you know it,
   clap your hands.
If you're happy and you know it,
   clap your hands.
If you're happy and you know it,
And you really want to show it,
If you're happy and you know it,
   clap your hands.

Stamp your feet! Shout hooray! Do all three!

39 Mother's Day

Suggested Books

Buckley, *Grandmother and I*
Bunting, *Flower Garden*
Jonas, *Two Bear Cubs*
Joosse, *Mama, Do You Love Me?*
Scott, *On Mother's Lap*

Opening Song

The More We Get Together

The music is in *Eye Winker, Tom Tinker . . .* and *The Raffi Singable Songbook*. This song can just be sung or you can add the finger-game aspects.

Verse 1: Hug yourself and sway side to side. Point both fingers to "your friends," then touch yourself on "my friends," then back to hugging.

Verse 2: Clasp hands and sway back and forth. Shake hands with person nearest you, or all hold hands.

Name Song and Finger Game

Charlie over the Water

The music is in *Eye Winker, Tom Tinker . . . .*

Point to everyone for the first two lines. Clap hands on "blackbird," then point to yourself for last line.

Opening Finger Game

Open, Shut Them

Suit actions to words.

Song

Hush, Little Baby

The music is in *Go In and Out the Window, Reader's Digest Children's Songbook,* and *Singing Bee!*

Finger Game

Fold Your Hands

Fold hands in front of you;
Lay them in lap;
Pick up book and show it.

Song and Finger Game

¿Donde Está?

Sung to the tune of "Frère Jacques." The music is in *The Baby's Song Book, Songs That Children Sing,* and *Singing Bee!*

Hold up hand and touch each member of the
    family when named;
For "hermanitos" touch the last three fingers
    one by one.

Tickle

The Bumblebee

Put forefinger and thumb together for the bee;
Fly bee around and tickle child anywhere at the
    "Buzzz!"

Closing Song

If You're Happy and You Know It

This well-known song and finger game can be found in *Do Your Ears Hang Low?* or *Ring a Ring o' Roses.* Suit actions to words, clapping and stamping twice, shouting "hooray" once, and repeating them all for "Do all three!"

Mother's Day

The More We Get Together
The more we get together, together, together,
The more we get together,
The happier we'll be.

For your friends are my friends
And my friends are your friends.
The more we get together,
The happier we'll be.

The more we share together,
Together, together,
The more we share together,
The happier we'll be.

For sharing is caring and caring is sharing,
The more we share together.
The happier we'll be.

Charlie over the Water
————— over the water,
————— over the sea,
————— catch a blackbird,
Can't catch me!

Open, Shut Them
Open, shut them; open, shut them;
Let your hands go clap, clap, clap.
Open, shut them; open, shut them;
Drop them in your lap, lap, lap.

Walk them, walk them, walk them, walk them,
Right up to your chin, chin, chin.
Open up your little mouth,
But do not let them in.

Book: _____

Hush, Little Baby
Hush, little baby, don't say a word,
Mama's gonna buy you a mockingbird.

If that mockingbird don't sing,
Mama's gonna buy you a diamond ring.

If that diamond ring turns brass,
Mama's gonna buy you a looking glass.

If that looking glass gets broke,
Mama's gonna buy you a billy goat.

If that billy goat won't pull,
Mama's gonna buy you a cart and bull.

If that cart and bull turn over,
Mama's gonna buy you a dog named Rover.

If that dog named Rover don't bark,
Mama's gonna buy you a horse and cart.

If that horse and cart fall down,
You'll still be the sweetest little baby in town.

Fold Your Hands
Fold your hands so quietly,
Fold your hands like this you see.
Ready for a special look?
I'm going to read a special book.

Book: _____

¿Donde Está?
¿Donde está, donde está
Mi familia, mi familia?

Aqui está mamá
Y tambien papá,
Y mis hermanitos,
Y mis hermanitos.

The Bumblebee
A bumblebee comes around the barn,
With a bundle of stingers under his arm.
Buzzzzzzzzzzzz!

If You're Happy and You Know It
If you're happy and you know it,
   clap your hands.
If you're happy and you know it,
   clap your hands.
If you're happy and you know it,
And you really want to show it,
If you're happy and you know it,
   clap your hands.

Stamp your feet! Shout hooray! Do all three!

40 Father's Day

Suggested Books

Asch, *Just like Daddy*
Buckley, *Grandfather and I*
Greenfield, *My Daddy and I*
Hill, *Spot Bakes a Cake*
Watanabe, *Where's My Daddy?*

Opening Song

The More We Get Together

The music is in *Eye Winker, Tom Tinker . . .* and *The Raffi Singable Songbook.* This song can just be sung or you can add the finger-game aspects.

Verse 1: Hug yourself and sway side to side. Point both fingers to "your friends," then touch yourself on "my friends," then back to hugging.

Verse 2: Clasp hands and sway back and forth. Shake hands with person nearest you, or all hold hands.

Name Song and Finger Game

Charlie over the Water

The music is in *Eye Winker, Tom Tinker . . . .*

Point to everyone for the first two lines. Clap hands on "blackbird," then point to yourself for last line.

Opening Finger Game

Open, Shut Them

Suit actions to words.

Poem

"Daddy," Said the Baby

Chant or rap while rhythmically clapping along. This can also be a lap jog.

Song

Hush, Little Baby

The music is in *Go In and Out the Window, Reader's Digest Children's Songbook,* and *Singing Bee!*

Finger Game

This Is My Father

Hold up hand and touch each finger in turn starting at the thumb;
Wrap hand in other and bring to chest at last line.

Lap Jog

Ride Away, Ride Away, Baby Shall Ride

Jog child on lap;
Others can clap along.

Closing Song

If You're Happy and You Know It

This well-known song and finger game can be found in *Do Your Ears Hang Low?* or *Ring a Ring o' Roses.* Suit actions to words, clapping and stamping twice, shouting "hooray" once, and repeating them all for "Do all three!"

Father's Day

The More We Get Together

The more we get together, together, together,
The more we get together,
The happier we'll be.

For your friends are my friends
And my friends are your friends.
The more we get together,
The happier we'll be.

The more we share together,
Together, together,
The more we share together,
The happier we'll be.

For sharing is caring and caring is sharing,
The more we share together,
The happier we'll be.

Charlie over the Water

———— over the water,
———— over the sea,
———— catch a blackbird,
Can't catch me!

Open, Shut Them

Open, shut them; open, shut them;
Let your hands go clap, clap, clap.
Open, shut them; open, shut them;
Drop them in your lap, lap, lap.

Walk them, walk them, walk them, walk them,
Right up to your chin, chin, chin.
Open up your little mouth,
But do not let them in.

Book: _____

"Daddy," Said the Baby

"Daddy," said the baby,
"Wonderful," said the Mom.
"Daddy," said the baby,
"Cute," said the son.

"Daddy," said the baby,
The sister looked intrigued.
"Daddy," said the baby,
And Daddy looked pleased.

Book: _____

Hush, Little Baby

Hush, little baby, don't say a word,
Papa's gonna buy you a mockingbird.

If that mockingbird don't sing,
Papa's gonna buy you a diamond ring.

If that diamond ring turns brass,
Papa's gonna buy you a looking glass.

If that looking glass gets broke,
Papa's gonna buy you a billy goat.

If that billy goat won't pull,
Papa's gonna buy you a cart and bull.

If that cart and bull turn over,
Papa's gonna buy you a dog named Rover.

If that dog named Rover don't bark,
Papa's gonna buy you a horse and cart.

If that horse and cart fall down,
You'll still be the sweetest little baby in town.

This Is My Father

This is my father, this is my mother,
This is my brother, tall;
This is my sister, this is the baby,
Oh! How I love them all.

Ride Away, Ride Away, Baby Shall Ride

Ride away, ride away, baby shall ride,
And have a wee puppy dog tied to one side,
A wee pussy cat shall be tied to the other,
And baby shall ride to her grandfather.

If You're Happy and You Know It

If you're happy and you know it,
   clap your hands.
If you're happy and you know it,
   clap your hands.
If you're happy and you know it,
And you really want to show it,
If you're happy and you know it,
   clap your hands.

Stamp your feet! Shout hooray! Do all three!

41 Fourth of July / Independence Day

Suggested Books

Crews, *Parade*
Florian, *A Beach Day*
———, *A Summer Day*
Hill, *Spot Goes to the Circus*

Opening Song

The More We Get Together

The music is in *Eye Winker, Tom Tinker . . .* and *The Raffi Singable Songbook.* This song can just be sung or you can add the finger-game aspects.

Verse 1: Hug yourself and sway side to side. Point both fingers to "your friends," then touch yourself on "my friends," then back to hugging.

Verse 2: Clasp hands and sway back and forth. Shake hands with person nearest you, or all hold hands.

Name Song and Finger Game

Charlie over the Water

The music is in *Eye Winker, Tom Tinker . . . .*

Point to everyone for the first two lines. Clap hands on "blackbird," then point to yourself for last line.

Opening Finger Game

Open, Shut Them

Suit actions to words.

Song

Yankee Doodle

The music is in *The Baby's Song Book, Go In and Out the Window,* and *Singing Bee!*

This song was used by the British to make fun of the Americans during the Revolutionary War. In the later years of the war, the Americans made it their own.

Song

Twinkle, Twinkle, Little Star

The music is in *Singing Bee!*

Song

America

The music is in *Go In and Out the Window.*

Foot Pat or Lap Jog

Shoe a Little Horse

Tap very young child's foot. Older children can enjoy a lap jog. Others can clap along.

Closing Song

If You're Happy and You Know It

This well-known song and finger game can be found in *Do Your Ears Hang Low?* or *Ring a Ring o' Roses.* Suit actions to words, clapping and stamping twice, shouting "hooray" once, and repeating them all for "Do all three!"

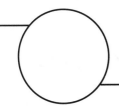

Fourth of July / Independence Day

The More We Get Together

The more we get together, together, together,
The more we get together,
The happier we'll be.

For your friends are my friends
And my friends are your friends.
The more we get together,
The happier we'll be.

The more we share together,
Together, together,
The more we share together,
The happier we'll be.

For sharing is caring and caring is sharing,
The more we share together,
The happier we'll be.

Charlie over the Water

———— over the water,
———— over the sea,
———— catch a blackbird,
Can't catch me!

Open, Shut Them

Open, shut them; open, shut them;
Let your hands go clap, clap, clap.
Open, shut them; open, shut them;
Drop them in your lap, lap, lap.

Walk them, walk them, walk them, walk them,
Right up to your chin, chin, chin.
Open up your little mouth,
But do not let them in.

Book: _____

Yankee Doodle

Yankee Doodle went to town,
Riding on a pony,
He stuck a feather in his cap
And called it macaroni!

Refrain:
Yankee Doodle, keep it up,
Yankee Doodle dandy;
Mind the music and the step,
And with the folks be handy!

Father and I went down to camp,
Along with Captain Good'in,
And there we saw the men and boys,
As thick as hasty puddin'.
(Repeat refrain.)

Book: _____

Twinkle, Twinkle, Little Star

Twinkle, twinkle, little star,
How I wonder what you are,
Up above the world so high,
Like a diamond in the sky.
Twinkle, twinkle, little star,
How I wonder what you are.

America

My country, 'tis of thee,
Sweet land of liberty,
Of thee I sing.
Land where my fathers
    died,
Land of the Pilgrim's
    pride,
From ev'ry mountain side,
Let freedom ring.

Shoe a Little Horse

Shoe a little horse,
Shoe a little mare,
But let the little colt
Go bare, bare, bare.

If You're Happy and You Know It

If you're happy and you know it,
    clap your hands.
If you're happy and you know it,
    clap your hands.
If you're happy and you know it,
And you really want to show it,
If you're happy and you know it,
    clap your hands.

Stamp your feet! Shout hooray! Do all three!

42 People Working / Labor Day

Suggested Books

Barton, *I Want to Be an Astronaut*
————, *Machines at Work*
Domanska, *Busy Monday Morning*
Field, *General Store*
Miller, *Whose Hat?*
————, *Whose Shoe?*
Paterson, *Soap and Suds*
Rice, *Sam Who Never Forgets*

Opening Song

The More We Get Together

The music is in *Eye Winker, Tom Tinker* . . . and *The Raffi Singable Songbook*. This song can just be sung or you can add the finger-game aspects.

Verse 1: Hug yourself and sway side to side. Point both fingers to "your friends," then touch yourself on "my friends," then back to hugging.

Verse 2: Clasp hands and sway back and forth. Shake hands with person nearest you, or all hold hands.

Name Song and Finger Game

Charlie over the Water

The music is in *Eye Winker, Tom Tinker* . . . .

Point to everyone for the first two lines. Clap hands on "blackbird," then point to yourself for last line.

Opening Finger Game

Open, Shut Them

Suit actions to words.

Song

Merrily We Work All Day

Sung to the tune "Mary Had a Little Lamb." The music is in *Singing Bee!*

Song

I've Been Working on the Railroad

The music can be found in *Singing Bee!* and *Songs America Sings*.

Lap Jog

To Market, To Market

Jog child on lap. Others can clap along.

Closing Song

If You're Happy and You Know It

This well-known song and finger game can be found in *Do Your Ears Hang Low?* or *Ring a Ring o' Roses*. Suit actions to words, clapping and stamping twice, shouting "hooray" once, and repeating them all for "Do all three!"

Other Suggestions

Try the song "Whistle While You Work," which is in the *Reader's Digest Children's Songbook*.

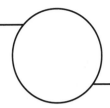

People Working / Labor Day

The More We Get Together
The more we get together, together, together,
The more we get together,
The happier we'll be.

For your friends are my friends
And my friends are your friends.
The more we get together,
The happier we'll be.

The more we share together,
Together, together,
The more we share together,
The happier we'll be.

For sharing is caring and caring is sharing,
The more we share together,
The happier we'll be.

Charlie over the Water
——— over the water,
——— over the sea,
——— catch a blackbird,
Can't catch me!

Open, Shut Them
Open, shut them; open, shut them;
Let your hands go clap, clap, clap.
Open, shut them; open, shut them;
Drop them in your lap, lap, lap.

Walk them, walk them, walk them, walk them,
Right up to your chin, chin, chin.
Open up your little mouth,
But do not let them in.

Book:
_____

Merrily We Work All Day
Merrily we work all day,
Work all day, work all day.
Merrily we work all day,
In the candy factory.

We make the best lollipops,
Lollipops, lollipops.
We make the best lollipops,
That you ever did see.

Book: _____

I've Been Working on the Railroad
I've been working on the railroad
All the live long day.
I've been working on the railroad,
Just to pass the time away.
Don't you hear the whistle blowing,
Rise up so early in the morn;
Don't you hear the captain shouting,
Dinah blow your horn.

Dinah won't you blow, Dinah won't you blow,
Dinah won't you blow your horn?
Dinah won't you blow, Dinah won't you blow,
Dinah won't you blow your horn?

Someone's in the kitchen with Dinah,
Someone's in the kitchen I know.
Someone's in the kitchen with Dinah,
Strumming on the old banjo.

Fe fi fiddle e-i-o, fe fi fiddle e-i-o,
Fe fi fiddle e-i-o,
Strumming on the old banjo.

To Market, To Market
To market, to market, to buy a fat pig.
Home again, home again, jiggity jig.

To market, to market, to buy a fat hog.
Home again, home again, jiggity jog.

If You're Happy and You Know It
If you're happy and you know it,
  clap your hands.
If you're happy and you know it,
  clap your hands.
If you're happy and you know it,
And you really want to show it,
If you're happy and you know it,
  clap your hands.

Stamp your feet! Shout hooray! Do all three!

43 Autumn and Halloween

Suggested Books
Dabcovich, *Sleepy Bear*
DePaola, *My First Halloween*
Hall, *It's Pumpkin Time*
Marshall, *Space Case*
Titherington, *Pumpkin, Pumpkin*

Opening Song
The More We Get Together

The music is in *Eye Winker, Tom Tinker* . . . and *The Raffi Singable Songbook*. This song can just be sung or you can add the finger-game aspects.

Verse 1: Hug yourself and sway side to side. Point both fingers to "your friends," then touch yourself on "my friends," then back to hugging.

Verse 2: Clasp hands and sway back and forth. Shake hands with person nearest you, or all hold hands.

Name Song and Finger Game
Charlie over the Water

The music is in *Eye Winker, Tom Tinker* . . . .

Point to everyone for the first two lines. Clap hands on "blackbird," then point to yourself for last line.

Opening Finger Game
Open, Shut Them

Suit actions to words.

Finger Game
What Am I?

Hands in circle;
Touch eyes;
Touch nose;
Touch mouth and grin;
Shake arms and legs;
One hand on head, the other on chin.

Song and Finger Game
Ten Little Witches

Sung to the tune "Ten Little Indians." The music is in *Eye Winker, Tom Tinker* . . . .

Hold up ten fingers;
Touch each finger in turn as you count up.

Finger Game
The Little Leaves

Raise hands and lower them, fluttering fingers like falling leaves;
Whirl hands as they flutter;
Touch floor.

Finger Game
Halloween Is Here

Make fingers walk;
Make goggles with hand and place around eyes;
Cup hands around mouth, saying "Whoooo!"
Flutter hands in air for flying witches;
Raise and lower hands slowly for ghosts;
Cup hand around mouth, saying "Oooo!"
Hug self in fear.

Song
Rockabye Baby

The music is in *The Lullaby Songbook* and *Singing Bee!*

Closing Song
If You're Happy and You Know It

This well-known song and finger game can be found in *Do Your Ears Hang Low?* or *Ring a Ring o' Roses*. Suit actions to words, clapping and stamping twice, shouting "hooray" once, and repeating them all for "Do all three!"

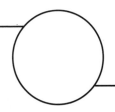

Autumn and Halloween

The More We Get Together
The more we get together, together, together,
The more we get together,
The happier we'll be.

For your friends are my friends
And my friends are your friends.
The more we get together,
The happier we'll be.

The more we share together,
Together, together,
The more we share together,
The happier we'll be.

For sharing is caring and caring is sharing,
The more we share together,
The happier we'll be.

Charlie over the Water
——— over the water,
——— over the sea,
——— catch a blackbird,
Can't catch me!

Open, Shut Them
Open, shut them; open, shut them;
Let your hands go clap, clap, clap.
Open, shut them; open, shut them;
Drop them in your lap, lap, lap.

Walk them, walk them, walk them, walk them,
Right up to your chin, chin, chin.
Open up your little mouth,
But do not let them in.

Book: _____

What Am I?
A face so round
And eyes so bright
A nose that glows,
My, what a sight.

A fiery mouth
With a jolly grin.
No arms! No legs!
Just head to chin.

What am I?
A jack-o-lantern.

Ten Little Witches
One little, two little, three little witches,
Four little, five little, six little witches,
Seven little, eight little, nine little witches,
Ten little witches on Halloween night.

One little, two little, three little black cats, . . .
One little, two little, three little ghosties, . . .

Book: _____

The Little Leaves
The little leaves are falling down,
Round and round, round and round.
The little leaves are falling down,
Falling to the ground.

Halloween Is Here
When goblins prowl,
And hoot owls howl,
Whoooo! Whoooo!
And pale ghosts sigh,
Oooo! Oooo!
Boys and girls, don't shake with fear,
It just means Halloween is near.

Rockabye Baby
Rockabye baby, on the tree top.
When the wind blows the cradle will rock;
When the bough breaks the cradle will fall;
Down will come baby, cradle and all.

If You're Happy and You Know It
If you're happy and you know it,
    clap your hands.
If you're happy and you know it,
    clap your hands.
If you're happy and you know it,
And you really want to show it,
If you're happy and you know it,
    clap your hands.

Stamp your feet! Shout hooray! Do all three!

44 Thanksgiving

Suggested Books

Child, *Over the River and through the Wood*
Ill. by Manson
———, *Over the River and through the Wood*
Ill. by Westcott
DePaola, *My First Thanksgiving*

Opening Song

The More We Get Together

The music is in *Eye Winker, Tom Tinker* . . . and *The Raffi Singable Songbook*. This song can just be sung or you can add the finger-game aspects.

Verse 1: Hug yourself and sway side to side. Point both fingers to "your friends," then touch yourself on "my friends," then back to hugging.

Verse 2: Clasp hands and sway back and forth. Shake hands with person nearest you, or all hold hands.

Name Song and Finger Game

Charlie over the Water

The music is in *Eye Winker, Tom Tinker* . . . .

Point to everyone for the first two lines. Clap hands on "blackbird," then point to yourself for last line.

Opening Finger Game

Open, Shut Them

Suit actions to words.

Song and Finger Game

Ten Little Pilgrims

Sung to the tune "Ten Little Indians." The music is in *Eye Winker, Tom Tinker* . . . .

Hold up fingers;
Touch each finger in turn as you count up and then down;
Rub stomach.

Song

Over the River and through the Wood

The music is in *Singing Bee!*

Lap Jog

Turkey and Gravy

Jog child on lap. Others can clap along.

Closing Song

If You're Happy and You Know It

This well-known song and finger game can be found in *Do Your Ears Hang Low?* or *Ring a Ring o' Roses*. Suit actions to words, clapping and stamping twice, shouting "hooray" once, and repeating them all for "Do all three!"

Thanksgiving

The More We Get Together

The more we get together, together, together,
The more we get together,
The happier we'll be.

For your friends are my friends
And my friends are your friends.
The more we get together,
The happier we'll be.

The more we share together,
Together, together,
The more we share together,
The happier we'll be.

For sharing is caring and caring is sharing,
The more we share together,
The happier we'll be.

Charlie over the Water

——— over the water,
——— over the sea,
——— catch a blackbird,
Can't catch me!

Open, Shut Them

Open, shut them; open, shut them;
Let your hands go clap, clap, clap.
Open, shut them; open, shut them;
Drop them in your lap, lap, lap.

Walk them, walk them, walk them,
    walk them,
Right up to your chin, chin, chin.
Open up your little mouth,
But do not let them in.

Book: _____

Ten Little Pilgrims

One little, two little, three little pilgrims,
Four little, five little, six little pilgrims,
Seven little, eight little, nine little pilgrims,
Ten little pilgrims came for dinner.

Ten little, nine little, eight little pilgrims, . . .
One little pilgrim ate too much.

Book: _____

Over the River and through the Wood

Over the river and through the wood
To Grandmother's house we go
The horse knows the way
To carry the sleigh
Through the white and drifted snow.

Over the river and through the wood
Oh how the wind does blow.
It stings the toes and bites the nose
As over the fields we go.

Over the river and through the wood
Trot fast my dapple gray.
Spring over the ground
Like a hunting hound
For this is Thanksgiving Day.

Over the river and through the wood
Now Grandmother's cap I spy.
Hooray for the fun
Is the pudding done?
Hooray for the pumpkin pie!

Turkey and Gravy

Turkey and gravy, turkey and gravy,
So good to eat.
Turkey and gravy, turkey and gravy,
What a wonderful treat.

Sweet potatoes, sweet potatoes, . . .
Cranberry sauce, cranberry sauce, . . .
Olives and pickles, olives and pickles, . . .
Pumpkin pie, pumpkin pie, . . .

If You're Happy and You Know It

If you're happy and you know it,
    clap your hands.
If you're happy and you know it,
    clap your hands.
If you're happy and you know it,
And you really want to show it,
If you're happy and you know it,
    clap your hands.

Stamp your feet! Shout hooray! Do all three!

Dreidels and Friends / Chanukah

Suggested Books
DePaola, *My First Chanukah*
Florian, *A Winter Day*

Opening Song
The More We Get Together

The music is in *Eye Winker, Tom Tinker* . . . and *The Raffi Singable Songbook*. This song can just be sung or you can add the finger-game aspects.

Verse 1: Hug yourself and sway side to side. Point both fingers to "your friends," then touch yourself on "my friends," then back to hugging.

Verse 2: Clasp hands and sway back and forth. Shake hands with person nearest you, or all hold hands.

Name Song and Finger Game
Charlie over the Water

The music is in *Eye Winker, Tom Tinker* . . . .

Point to everyone for the first two lines. Clap hands on "blackbird," then point to yourself for last line.

Opening Finger Game
Open, Shut Them

Suit actions to words.

Song
My Dreidel

The music is in *The Raffi Singable Songbook* under the title "My Dreydel."

Finger Game
Eight Little Candles

Hold up eight fingers, then seven, etc.

Song
The Muffin Man / The Latke Man

The music is in *Singing Bee!*

Closing Song
If You're Happy and You Know It

This well-known song and finger game can be found in *Do Your Ears Hang Low?* or *Ring a Ring o' Roses*. Suit actions to words, clapping and stamping twice, shouting "hooray" once, and repeating them all for "Do all three!"

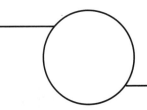

Dreidels and Friends / Chanukah

The More We Get Together

The more we get together, together, together,
The more we get together,
The happier we'll be.

For your friends are my friends
And my friends are your friends.
The more we get together,
The happier we'll be.

The more we share together,
Together, together,
The more we share together,
The happier we'll be.

For sharing is caring and caring is sharing,
The more we share together,
The happier we'll be.

Charlie over the Water

———— over the water,
———— over the sea,
———— catch a blackbird,
Can't catch me!

Open, Shut Them

Open, shut them; open, shut them;
Let your hands go clap, clap, clap.
Open, shut them; open, shut them;
Drop them in your lap, lap, lap.

Walk them, walk them, walk them, walk them,
Right up to your chin, chin, chin.
Open up your little mouth,
But do not let them in.

Book: _____

My Dreidel

I have a little dreidel,
I made it out of clay.
And when it's dry and ready,
Then dreidel I will play.

Refrain:
Oh, dreidel, dreidel, dreidel!
I made it out of clay.
And when it's dry and ready,
Then dreidel I will play.

It has a lovely body,
A leg so short and thin.
And when it gets all tired,
It drops and then I win.
(Repeat refrain.)

Book: _____

Eight Little Candles

Eight little candles,
Sitting on the menorah.
One jumped off and
    danced the horah.

Seven . . .
Six . . .
Five . . .
Four . . .
Three . . .
Two . . .
One . . .

The Muffin Man/The Latke Man

Oh do you know the muffin man
The muffin man, the muffin man,
Oh do you know the muffin man
Who lived in Drury Lane?

He ran off with the dairy maid
The dairy maid, the dairy maid,
He ran off the with dairy maid,
Who lived in Drury lane.

Oh now we have the latke man
The latke man, the latke man,
Oh now we have the latke man,
He's here for Chanukah.

If You're Happy and You Know It

If you're happy and you know it,
    clap your hands.
If you're happy and you know it,
    clap your hands.
If you're happy and you know it,
And you really want to show it,
If you're happy and you know it,
    clap your hands.

Stamp your feet! Shout hooray! Do all three!

46 Christmas Is Coming

Suggested Books

DePaola, *Baby's First Christmas*
Florian, *A Winter Day*
Hill, *Spot's First Christmas*
Wells, *Max's Christmas*

Opening Song

The More We Get Together

The music is in *Eye Winker, Tom Tinker . . .* and *The Raffi Singable Songbook*. This song can just be sung or you can add the finger-game aspects.

Verse 1: Hug yourself and sway side to side. Point both fingers to "your friends," then touch yourself on "my friends," then back to hugging.

Verse 2: Clasp hands and sway back and forth. Shake hands with person nearest you, or all hold hands.

Name Song and Finger Game

Charlie over the Water

The music is in *Eye Winker, Tom Tinker . . . .*

Point to everyone for the first two lines. Clap hands on "blackbird," then point to yourself for last line.

Opening Finger Game

Open, Shut Them

Suit actions to words.

Song

We Wish You a Merry Christmas

The music is in *Singing Bee!*

Song

Jingle Bells

The music is in *Do Your Ears Hang Low?* and *Singing Bee!*

Song and Lap Jog

Santa Claus Is Coming

Sung to the tune "Christmas Is Coming."

Jog child in lap while singing, chanting, or
rapping;
Others can clap along.

Closing Song

If You're Happy and You Know It

This well-known song and finger game can be found in *Do Your Ears Hang Low?* or *Ring a Ring o' Roses*. Suit actions to words, clapping and stamping twice, shouting "hooray" once, and repeating them all for "Do all three!"

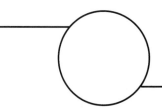

Christmas Is Coming

The More We Get Together
The more we get together, together, together,
The more we get together,
The happier we'll be.

For your friends are my friends
And my friends are your friends.
The more we get together,
The happier we'll be.

The more we share together,
Together, together,
The more we share together,
The happier we'll be.

For sharing is caring and caring is sharing,
The more we share together,
The happier we'll be.

Charlie over the Water
——— over the water,
——— over the sea,
——— catch a blackbird,
Can't catch me!

Open, Shut Them
Open, shut them; open, shut them;
Let your hands go clap, clap, clap.
Open, shut them; open, shut them;
Drop them in your lap, lap, lap.

Walk them, walk them, walk them, walk them,
Right up to your chin, chin, chin.
Open up your little mouth,
But do not let them in.

Book: _____

We Wish You a Merry Christmas
We wish you a Merry Christmas,
We wish you a Merry Christmas,
We wish you a Merry Christmas,
And a Happy New Year!

Now bring us some figgy pudding, . . .
And bring it right here!

We won't go until we get some, . . .
So bring it out here!
(Repeat first verse.)

Book: _____

Jingle Bells
Dashing through the snow
In a one-horse open sleigh,
O'er the fields we go,
Laughing all the way;
Bells on bob-tail ring,
Making spirits bright,
What fun it is to ride and sing
A sleighing song tonight!

Refrain:
Jingle bells, jingle bells!
Jingle all the way!
Oh what fun it is to ride
In a one-horse open sleigh!
(Repeat once.)

A day or two ago,
I thought I'd take a ride,
And soon Miss Fanny Bright
Was seated by my side;
The horse was lean and lank;
Misfortune seemed his lot;
He got into a drifted bank,
And we, we got upsot!
(Repeat refrain.)

Santa Claus Is Coming
Santa Claus is coming,
I'm very sure of that.
He wears a bright red suit,
And a floppy hat.

I asked for something special,
I wrote a letter, too.
I got a rocking horse,
Now I'm a BOUNCING BUCKAROO!

If You're Happy and You Know It
If you're happy and you know it,
    clap your hands.
If you're happy and you know it,
    clap your hands.
If you're happy and you know it,
And you really want to show it,
If you're happy and you know it,
    clap your hands.

Stamp your feet! Shout hooray! Do all three!

47 Kwanzaa

Suggested Books

Falwell, *Feast for Ten*
Lewin, *Jafta*
Any book in the picture book bibliography
with African-American characters.

Opening Song

The More We Get Together

The music is in *Eye Winker, Tom Tinker* . . . and
The Raffi Singable Songbook. This song can just
be sung or you can add the finger-game aspects.

Verse 1: Hug yourself and sway side to side.
Point both fingers to "your friends," then touch
yourself on "my friends," then back to hugging.

Verse 2: Clasp hands and sway back and forth.
Shake hands with person nearest you, or all
hold hands.

Name Song and Finger Game

Charlie over the Water

The music is in *Eye Winker, Tom Tinker* . . . .

Point to everyone for the first two lines. Clap
hands on "blackbird," then point to yourself for
last line.

Opening Finger Game

Open, Shut Them

Suit actions to words.

Finger Game

Light a Candle on the Kinara

Hold up one finger and touch it;
Hold up six fingers;
Repeat touching one finger and holding up
    decreasing number of fingers;
Hold up seven fingers for last verse.

Song

This Little Light of Mine

The music is in *Lift Every Voice and Sing* and
Songs of Peace, Freedom and Protest.

Lap Jog

Boing! Boing! Squeak!

This poem by Jack Prelutsky can be found in
his collection, *New Kid on the Block*. It also
happens to make a great lap jog. This has been
a favorite for years among infant-toddler
programmers and their audiences. Enjoy.

Closing Song

If You're Happy and You Know It

This well-known song and finger game can be
found in *Do Your Ears Hang Low?* or *Ring a Ring
o' Roses*. Suit actions to words, clapping and
stamping twice, shouting "hooray" once, and
repeating them all for "Do all three!"

Kwanzaa

The More We Get Together

The more we get together, together, together,
The more we get together,
The happier we'll be.

For your friends are my friends
And my friends are your friends.
The more we get together,
The happier we'll be.

The more we share together,
Together, together,
The more we share together,
The happier we'll be.

For sharing is caring and caring is sharing,
The more we share together,
The happier we'll be.

Charlie over the Water

——— over the water,
——— over the sea,
——— catch a blackbird,
Can't catch me!

Open, Shut Them

Open, shut them; open, shut them;
Let your hands go clap, clap, clap.
Open, shut them; open, shut them;
Drop them in your lap, lap, lap.

Walk them, walk them, walk them, walk them,
Right up to your chin, chin, chin.
Open up your little mouth,
But do not let them in.

Book: _____

Light a Candle on the Kinara

Light a candle on the kinara
See how it glows
Now there are six left to light
All sitting in a row.

. . . Now there are five left to light . . .
. . . Now there are four left to light . . .
. . . Now there are three left to light . . .
. . . Now there are two left to light . . .
. . . Now there is one left to light . . .

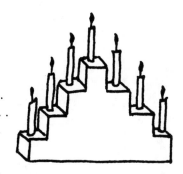

The candles are lit on the kinara
See how they glow
The seven days of Kwanzaa
All sitting in a row.

Book: _____

This Little Light of Mine

This little light of mine
I'm gonna let it shine,
This little light of mine
I'm gonna let it shine,
This little light of mine
I'm gonna let it shine.
Let it shine, let it shine, let it shine.

Everywhere I go . . .
All through the night . . .

Boing! Boing! Squeak!

Refrain:
Boing! Boing! Squeak!
Boing! Boing! Squeak!
A bouncing mouse is in my house,
It's been here for a week.

It bounced from out of nowhere,
Then quickly settled in,
I'm grateful that it came alone
(I've heard it has a twin),
It bounces in the kitchen,
It bounces in the den,
It bounces through the living room—
Look! There it goes again.
(Repeat refrain.)

If You're Happy and You Know It

If you're happy and you know it,
  clap your hands.
If you're happy and you know it,
  clap your hands.
If you're happy and you know it,
And you really want to show it,
If you're happy and you know it,
  clap your hands.

Stamp your feet! Shout hooray!
  Do all three!

48 Happy Birthday

Suggested Books

Bornstein, *Little Gorilla*
Bunting, *Flower Garden*
Hill, *Spot's Birthday Party*
Hutchins, *Happy Birthday, Sam*
Rice, *Benny Bakes a Cake*
Wells, *Max's Birthday*
Yolen, *Mouse's Birthday*

Opening Song

The More We Get Together

The music is in *Eye Winker, Tom Tinker*... and *The Raffi Singable Songbook*. This song can just be sung or you can add the finger-game aspects.

Verse 1: Hug yourself and sway side to side. Point both fingers to "your friends," then touch yourself on "my friends," then back to hugging.

Verse 2: Clasp hands and sway back and forth. Shake hands with person nearest you, or all hold hands.

Name Song and Finger Game

Charlie over the Water

The music is in *Eye Winker, Tom Tinker*....

Point to everyone for the first two lines. Clap hands on "blackbird," then point to yourself for last line.

Opening Finger Game

Open, Shut Them

Suit actions to words.

Finger Game

What Am I Baking?

Suit actions to words.

Finger Game

Clap Your Hands

Suit action to words.

The "Birthday Song"

Find someone in the audience, child or parent, who just had or will have a birthday and sing "Happy Birthday" to them.

Song

Oh, I Live in San Francisco

This is sung to the tune "Oh, Susanna." The music is in *Singing Bee!* and *Songs America Sings*.

This song can be lots of fun. It can be personalized by changing the child's age and where he or she lives. Instead of San Francisco, New York City or Mississippi or any number of names can be used. Have fun.

Finger Game

Chocolate

Chant rhythmically stressing each syllable. Remember, because it is Spanish, the *e* is pronounced like a long *a*.

Rub palms together to represent rotating the handle of a molinillo to mix chocolate into milk.

Closing Song

If You're Happy and You Know It

This well-known song and finger game can be found in *Do Your Ears Hang Low?* or *Ring a Ring o' Roses*. Suit actions to words, clapping and stamping twice, shouting "hooray" once, and repeating them all for "Do all three!"

Happy Birthday

The More We Get Together

The more we get together, together, together,
The more we get together,
The happier we'll be.

For your friends are my friends
And my friends are your friends.
The more we get together,
The happier we'll be.

The more we share together,
Together, together,
The more we share together,
The happier we'll be.

For sharing is caring and caring is sharing,
The more we share together,
The happier we'll be.

Charlie over the Water

———— over the water,
———— over the sea,
———— catch a blackbird,
Can't catch me!

Open, Shut Them

Open, shut them; open, shut them;
Let your hands go clap, clap, clap.
Open, shut them; open, shut them;
Drop them in your lap, lap, lap.

Walk them, walk them, walk them, walk them,
Right up to your chin, chin, chin.
Open up your little mouth,
But do not let them in.

Book: _____

What Am I Baking?

Sift the flour and break an egg.
Add some salt and a bit of
    nutmeg.
A spoon of butter, a cup
    of milk.
Stir and beat as fine as
    silk.
Want to know what
    I'm going to bake?
Shhhhh, it's a secret.
It's a birthday cake!

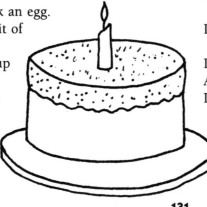

Clap Your Hands

Clap your hands, clap your hands,
Clap them just like me.
Touch your knees, touch your knees,
Touch them just like me.
Touch your feet, touch your feet,
Touch them just like me.
Clap your hands, clap you hands,
Now let them quiet be.

Book: _____

Oh, I Live in San Francisco

Oh, I live in San Francisco
And I'm three years old today.
I'm going to have a party,
And this is what I say.
No more naps, oh no more naps, no way.
For I live in San Francisco
And I'm three years old today.

Chocolate

Uno, dos, tres, cho-,
Uno, dos, tres, co-,
Uno, dos, tres, La,
Uno, dos, tres, Te.
Cho-co-la-te,
Cho-co-la-te,
Bate, bate, chocolate.
Cho-co-la-te,
Cho-co-la-te,
Bate, bate, chocolate.
Bate, bate, chocolate.
Bate, bate, bate, bate.

If You're Happy and You Know It

If you're happy and you know it,
    clap your hands.
If you're happy and you know it,
    clap your hands.
If you're happy and you know it,
And you really want to show it,
If you're happy and you know it,
    clap your hands.

Stamp your feet! Shout hooray! Do all three!

49 Let Us Rejoice

Suggested Books

Carlson, *I Like Me*
Charles, *What Am I?*
Crews, *Parade*
Degan, *Jamberry*
Greenfield, *I Make Music*
Raschka, *Yo! Yes?*

Opening Song

The More We Get Together

The music is in *Eye Winker, Tom Tinker* . . . and *The Raffi Singable Songbook*. This song can just be sung or you can add the finger-game aspects.

Verse 1: Hug yourself and sway side to side. Point both fingers to "your friends," then touch yourself on "my friends," then back to hugging.

Verse 2: Clasp hands and sway back and forth. Shake hands with person nearest you, or all hold hands.

Name Song and Finger Game

Charlie over the Water

The music is in *Eye Winker, Tom Tinker* . . . .

Point to everyone for the first two lines. Clap hands on "blackbird," then point to yourself for last line.

Opening Finger Game

Open, Shut Them

Suit actions to words.

Song

When the Saints . . .

The music is in *I'm Going to Sing*.

Finger Game

Fold Your Hands

Fold hands in front of you;
Lay them in lap;
Pick up book and show it.

Song

Hava Nagila

The music is in *Songs America Sings*. The Hebrew words of the title translate to "Let us rejoice." This song usually goes with a popular Israeli folk dance.

Finger Game

Tickle You Here

Hug child;
Gently tickle child;
Jog child on lap.

Closing Song

If You're Happy and You Know It

This well-known song and finger game can be found in *Do Your Ears Hang Low?* or *Ring a Ring o' Roses*. Suit actions to words, clapping and stamping twice, shouting "hooray" once, and repeating them all for "Do all three!"

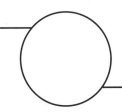

Let Us Rejoice

The More We Get Together

The more we get together, together, together,
The more we get together,
The happier we'll be.

For your friends are my friends
And my friends are your friends.
The more we get together,
The happier we'll be.

The more we share together,
Together, together,
The more we share together,
The happier we'll be.

For sharing is caring and caring is sharing,
The more we share together,
The happier we'll be.

Charlie over the Water

———— over the water,
———— over the sea,
———— catch a blackbird,
Can't catch me!

Open, Shut Them

Open, shut them; open, shut them;
Let your hands go clap, clap, clap.
Open, shut them; open, shut them;
Drop them in your lap, lap, lap.

Walk them, walk them, walk them, walk them,
Right up to your chin, chin, chin.
Open up your little mouth,
But do not let them in.

Book: _____

When the Saints . . .

Oh when the saints go marching in,
Oh when the saints go marching in,
I still want to be in that number
When the saints go marching in.

Oh when the stars have disappeared,
Oh when the stars have disappeared,
I still want to be in that number
When the saints go marching in.

Fold Your Hands

Fold your hands so quietly,
Fold your hands like this you see.
Ready for a special look?
I'm going to read a special book.

Book: _____

Hava Nagila

Hava nagila, hava nagila, hava nagila,
    v'nism'cha.
Hava nagila, hava nagila, hava nagila,
    v'nism'cha.
Hava n'ran'na, hava n'ran'na,
Hava n'ran'na, v'nism'cha.
Hava n'ran'na, hava n'ran'na,
Hava n'ran'na, v'nism'cha.

Uru, uru achim, uru achim b'lev sameach,
Uru achim b'lev sameach,
Uru achim b'lev sameach,
Uru achim b'lev sameach,
Uru achim! Uru achim! B'lev sameach!

Tickle You Here

Hug you here, hug you there,
Hug you, hug you everywhere.

Tickle you here, tickle you there,
Tickle you, tickle you everywhere.

Bounce you here, bounce you there,
Bounce you, bounce you everywhere.

If You're Happy and You Know It

If you're happy and you know it,
    clap your hands.
If you're happy and you know it,
    clap your hands.
If you're happy and you know it,
And you really want to show it,
If you're happy and you know it,
    clap your hands.

Stamp your feet! Shout hooray! Do all three!

50 People Soup

Suggested Books

Allen, *Bertie and the Bear*
Berger, *Grandfather Twilight*
Burningham, *Mr. Gumpy's Motor Car*
———, *Mr. Gumpy's Outing*
Carlson, *I Like Me*
Miller, *Whose Hat?*
———, *Whose Shoe?*
Morris, *Bread, Bread, Bread*
———, *Hats, Hats, Hats*
———, *Houses and Homes*
Roffey, *Grand Old Duke of York*

Opening Song

The More We Get Together

The music is in *Eye Winker, Tom Tinker . . .* and *The Raffi Singable Songbook*. This song can just be sung or you can add the finger-game aspects.

Verse 1: Hug yourself and sway side to side. Point both fingers to "your friends," then touch yourself on "my friends," then back to hugging.

Verse 2: Clasp hands and sway back and forth. Shake hands with person nearest you, or all hold hands.

Name Song and Finger Game

Charlie over the Water

The music is in *Eye Winker, Tom Tinker . . . .*

Point to everyone for the first two lines. Clap hands on "blackbird," then point to yourself for last line.

Opening Finger Game

Open, Shut Them

Suit actions to words.

Song

Yankee Doodle

The music is in *Go In and Out the Window*, *Reader's Digest Children's Songbook*, and *Singing Bee!*

Lap Jog

Ride a Cock-Horse

Jog child on lap. Others can clap along.

Song

Oh, Susanna!

The music is in *Go In and Out the Window* and *Singing Bee!* Written by Stephen Foster, this song became a hit in minstrel shows and later a theme song for the Forty-niners during the California gold rush.

Tickle

The Bumblebee

Put forefinger and thumb together for the bee. Fly bee around and then tickle child anywhere at the end of the "buzzzz!"

Closing Song

If You're Happy and You Know It

This well-known song and finger game can be found in *Do Your Ears Hang Low?* or *Ring a Ring o' Roses*. Suit actions to words, clapping and stamping twice, shouting "hooray" once, and repeating them all for "Do all three!"

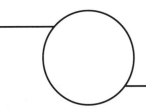

People Soup

The More We Get Together

The more we get together, together, together,
The more we get together,
The happier we'll be.

For your friends are my friends
And my friends are your friends.
The more we get together,
The happier we'll be.

The more we share together,
Together, together,
The more we share together,
The happier we'll be.

For sharing is caring and caring is sharing,
The more we share together,
The happier we'll be.

Charlie over the Water

—— over the water,
—— over the sea,
—— catch a blackbird,
Can't catch me!

Open, Shut Them

Open, shut them; open, shut them;
Let your hands go clap, clap, clap.
Open, shut them; open, shut them;
Drop them in your lap, lap, lap.

Walk them, walk them, walk them, walk them,
Right up to your chin, chin, chin.
Open up your little mouth,
But do not let them in.

Book: _____

Yankee Doodle

Yankee Doodle went to town,
Riding on a pony,
He stuck a feather in his cap
And called it macaroni!

Refrain:
Yankee Doodle, keep it up,
Yankee Doodle dandy;
Mind the music and the step,
And with the folks be handy!

Father and I went down to camp,
Along with Captain Good'in,

And there we saw the men and boys,
As thick as hasty puddin'.
(Repeat refrain.)

And there was Captain Washington
Upon a slapping stallion,
A-giving orders to his men,
I guess there was a million.
(Repeat refrain.)

Book: _____

Ride a Cock-Horse

Ride a cock horse to Banbury Cross
To see a fine lady upon a white horse.
Rings on her finger and bells on her toes,
She shall have music wherever she goes.

Oh, Susanna!

I come from Alabama
With a banjo on my knee;
I'm going to Lou'siana,
My true love for to see.

It rained all night the day I left,
The weather it was dry;
The sun so hot I froze to death,
Susanna, don't you cry.

Oh, Susanna! Oh don't you cry
    for me.
I come from Alabama
With my banjo on my knee.

The Bumblebee

A bumblebee comes around the barn,
With a bundle of stingers under his arm.
Buzzzzzzzzzzzzzz!

If You're Happy and You Know It

If you're happy and you know it,
    clap your hands.
If you're happy and you know it,
    clap your hands.
If you're happy and you know it,
And you really want to show it,
If you're happy and you know it,
    clap your hands.

Stamp your feet! Shout hooray! Do all three!

51 Potpourri

Suggested Books

Asch, *Moon Bear's Books*
Jorgensen, *Crocodile Beat*
Martin, *Chicka Chicka Boom Boom*
Any favorite picture book.

Opening Song

The More We Get Together

The music is in *Eye Winker, Tom Tinker . . .* and *The Raffi Singable Songbook.* This song can just be sung or you can add the finger-game aspects.

Verse 1: Hug yourself and sway side to side. Point both fingers to "your friends," then touch yourself on "my friends," then back to hugging.

Verse 2: Clasp hands and sway back and forth. Shake hands with person nearest you, or all hold hands.

Name Song and Finger Game

Charlie over the Water

The music is in *Eye Winker, Tom Tinker . . . .*

Point to everyone for the first two lines. Clap hands on "blackbird," then point to yourself for last line.

Opening Finger Game

Open, Shut Them

Suit actions to words.

Finger Game

Five Little Babies

Hold up five fingers and touch thumb;
Rocking motion with arms and hands;
Touch thumb and forefinger;
Splashing motion;
Touch thumb, forefinger and middle finger;
Crawling motion with hands and arms;
Touch four fingers;
Pounding motion with fist;
Touch all five fingers one by one;
Cover eyes and peek.

Finger Game

Fold Your Hands

Fold hands in front of you;
Lay them in lap;
Pick up book and show it.

Song

Pop! Goes the Weasel

The music is in *The Fireside Song Book of Birds and Beasts, Eye Winker, Tom Tinker . . . ,* and *Singing Bee!*

Lap Jog

I'm Bouncing

Jog child on lap;
On last line, open legs and lower child;
Others can clap along.

Closing Song

If You're Happy and You Know It

This well-known song and finger game can be found in *Do Your Ears Hang Low?* or *Ring a Ring o' Roses.* Suit actions to words, clapping and stamping twice, shouting "hooray" once, and repeating them all for "Do all three!"

Potpourri

The More We Get Together

The more we get together, together, together,
The more we get together,
The happier we'll be.

For your friends are my friends
And my friends are your friends.
The more we get together,
The happier we'll be.

The more we share together,
Together, together,
The more we share together,
The happier we'll be.

For sharing is caring and caring is sharing,
The more we share together,
The happier we'll be.

Charlie over the Water

———— over the water,
———— over the sea,
———— catch a blackbird,
Can't catch me!

Open, Shut Them

Open, shut them; open, shut them;
Let your hands go clap, clap, clap.
Open, shut them; open, shut them;
Drop them in your lap, lap, lap.

Walk them, walk them, walk them, walk them,
Right up to your chin, chin, chin.
Open up your little mouth,
But do not let them in.

Book: _____

Five Little Babies

One little baby
Rocking in a tree.
Two little babies
Splashing in the sea.
Three little babies
Crawling on the floor.
Four little babies
Banging on the door.
Five little babies
Playing hide and seek.
Keep your eyes closed tight, now,
Until I say . . . . Peek!

Fold Your Hands

Fold your hands so quietly.
Fold your hands like this you see.
Ready for a special look?
I'm going to read a special book.

Book: _____

Pop! Goes the Weasel

All around the cobbler's bench
The monkey chased the weasel.
The monkey thought 'twas all in fun.
Pop! Goes the weasel.

I've no time to sit and sigh,
No patience to wait till time goes by;
Kiss me quick, I'm off, good-bye,
Pop! Goes the weasel.

A penny for a spool of thread
A penny for a needle,
That's the way the money goes,
Pop! Goes the weasel.

I'm Bouncing

I'm bouncing, bouncing everywhere.
I bounce and bounce into the air.
I'm bouncing, bouncing like a ball.
I bounce and bounce, then down I fall.

If You're Happy and You Know It

If you're happy and you know it,
    clap your hands.
If you're happy and you know it,
    clap your hands.
If you're happy and you know it,
And you really want to show it,
If you're happy and you know it,
    clap your hands.

Stamp your feet! Shout hooray! Do all three!

52 Simply Silly

Suggested Books

Allen, *Who Sank the Boat?*
Janovitz, *Look Out, Bird!*
Martin, *Chicka Chicka Boom Boom*
Shaw, *Sheep in a Jeep*
————, *Sheep on a Ship*
————, *Sheep out to Eat*

Opening Song

The More We Get Together

The music is in *Eye Winker, Tom Tinker* . . . and *The Raffi Singable Songbook.* This song can just be sung or you can add the finger-game aspects.

Verse 1: Hug yourself and sway side to side. Point both fingers to "your friends," then touch yourself on "my friends," then back to hugging.

Verse 2: Clasp hands and sway back and forth. Shake hands with person nearest you, or all hold hands.

Name Song and Finger Game

Charlie over the Water

The music is in *Eye Winker, Tom Tinker* . . . .

Point to everyone for the first two lines. Clap hands on "blackbird," then point to yourself for last line.

Opening Finger Game

Open, Shut Them

Suit actions to words.

Song

Pop! Goes the Weasel

The music is in *Eye Winker, Tom Tinker* . . . , *Fireside Song Book of Birds and Beasts,* and *Singing Bee.*

Finger Game

Fold Your Hands

Fold hands in front of you;
Lay them in lap;
Pick up book and show it.

Lap Jog

Boing! Boing! Squeak!

This poem by Jack Prelutsky can be found in his collection, *New Kid on the Block.* It also happens to make a great lap jog. This has been a favorite for years among infant-toddler programmers and their audiences. Enjoy.

Closing Song

If You're Happy and You Know It

This well-known song and finger game can be found in *Do Your Ears Hang Low?* or *Ring a Ring o' Roses.* Suit actions to words, clapping and stamping twice, shouting "hooray" once, and repeating them all for "Do all three!"

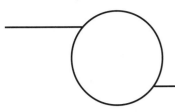

Simply Silly

The More We Get Together

The more we get together, together, together,
The more we get together,
The happier we'll be.

For your friends are my friends
And my friends are your friends.
The more we get together,
The happier we'll be.

The more we share together,
Together, together,
The more we share together,
The happier we'll be.

For sharing is caring and caring is sharing,
The more we share together,
The happier we'll be.

Charlie over the Water

——— over the water,
——— over the sea,
——— catch a blackbird,
Can't catch me!

Open, Shut Them

Open, shut them; open, shut them;
Let your hands go clap, clap, clap.
Open, shut them; open, shut them;
Drop them in your lap, lap, lap.

Walk them, walk them, walk them, walk them,
Right up to your chin, chin, chin.
Open up your little mouth,
But do not let them in.

Book: _____

Pop! Goes the Weasel

All around the cobbler's bench
The monkey chased the weasel.
The monkey thought 'twas all in fun.
Pop! Goes the weasel.

I've no time to sit and sigh,
No patience to wait till time goes by;
Kiss me quick, I'm off, good-bye,
Pop! Goes the weasel.

A penny for a spool of thread
A penny for a needle,

That's the way the money goes,
Pop! Goes the weasel.

Fold Your Hands

Fold your hands so quietly,
Fold your hands like this you see.
Ready for a special look?
I'm going to read a special book.

Book: _____

Boing! Boing! Squeak!

Refrain:
Boing! Boing! Squeak!
Boing! Boing! Squeak!
A bouncing mouse is in my house,
It's been here for a week.

It bounced from out of nowhere,
Then quickly settled in,
I'm grateful that it came alone
(I've heard it has a twin),
It bounces in the kitchen,
It bounces in the den,
It bounces through the living room—
Look! There it goes again.
(Repeat refrain.)

It bounces on the sofa,
On the table and the bed,
Up the stairs and on the chairs,
And even on my head,
That mouse continues bouncing
Every minute of the day.
It bounces, bounces, bounces,
But it doesn't bounce away.
(Repeat refrain.)

If You're Happy and You Know It

If you're happy and you know it,
    clap your hands.
If you're happy and you know it,
    clap your hands.
If you're happy and you know it,
And you really want to show it,
If you're happy and you know it,
    clap your hands.

Stamp your feet! Shout hooray! Do all three!

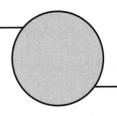

Bibliography of Picture Books

The following bibliography contains many tried and true books to use in baby-toddler programs. Each book is a suggested selection for one or more of the programs in Part 2 of this book. Keep in mind, however, that new and wonderful books are coming out every day. By choosing appropriate books and reading them well, you demonstrate the magic of the picture book experience. BB indicates a board book.

For sources of books in other languages, please consult the Multilingual and Multicultural Resources bibliography at the back of this book.

Allen, Pamela. *Bertie and the Bear*. New York: Coward McCann, 1984.

A boy is chased by a bear who is in turn chased by a Queen, an Admiral, etc., each making a different noise. This is a great participation book.

———. *Who Sank the Boat?* New York: Putnam, 1991.

A humorous rhyming text tells the story of a boat getting lower in the water as different animals gets in.

Arnosky, Jim. *Deer at the Brook*. New York: Lothrop, 1986.

A quiet nature study of deer and fawns at a brook.

———. *Every Autumn Comes the Bear*. New York: Putnam, 1993.

A bear finds a home for winter in this beautiful nature story.

Asch, Frank. *The Earth and I*. San Diego, Calif.: Harcourt Brace, 1994.

A child relates his special relationship with the earth and nature.

———. *Just like Daddy*. New York: Simon & Schuster, 1984.

A young anthropomorphic bear boy copies everything his Daddy does until the surprise ending.

———. *Moon Bear's Books*. New York: Simon & Schuster, 1993. (BB)

Moon Bear loves books and reading. One of a series of four.

———. *Turtle Tale*. New York: Dial, 1978.

A turtle can't make up his mind whether to keep his head in or out.

Bang, Molly. *Ten, Nine, Eight*. New York: Greenwillow, 1983.

A warm and simple rhyming counting book featuring an African-American father and daughter.

Barton, Byron. *Dinosaurs, Dinosaurs*. New York: HarperCollins, 1991.

The usual Barton treatment, but with popular dinosaurs as the subject.

———. *I Want to Be an Astronaut*. New York: HarperCollins, 1988.

Simple bold illustrations and text tell of a young child's wish to be an astronaut.

———. *Machines at Work*. New York: HarperCollins, 1987.

A crew of men and women are shown operating heavy equipment. Told with bright simple pictures and a simple text.

Berger, Barbara. *Grandfather Twilight*. New York: Philomel, 1986.

A beautiful and quiet story in which Grandfather Twilight takes a pearl and turns it into the moon.

Berry, Holly. *Old MacDonald Had a Farm*. New York: North-South, 1994.

A wonderful version of this popular song, in which each two-page spread presents another animal. The music is included.

Blumenthal, Nancy. *Count-a-Saurus*. Ill. Robert Kaufman. New York: Four Winds Press, 1989.

Big bright dinosaurs meet a counting book format sure to please young dinosaur lovers.

Bornstein, Ruth. *Little Gorilla*. New York: Clarion, 1986.

A young gorilla is loved by all the animals in the forest even as he becomes big and celebrates his first birthday.

Bradman, Tony. *Bad Babies' Book of Color*. Ill. Debbie Van der Beek. New York: Knopf, 1987.

A popular book that features photographs of babies.

———. *Bad Babies' Counting Book*. Ill. Debbie Van der Beek. New York: Knopf, 1986.

Photographs of babies misbehaving make this a popular counting book.

Brown, Margaret Wise. *Goodnight Moon*. Ill. Clement Hurd. New York: HarperCollins, 1947.

The classic story of a rabbit child saying goodnight to all the familiar things in his room.

Brown, Ruth. *Our Cat Flossie*. New York: Dutton, 1986.

A family cat's activities are shown with lovely illustrations and quiet text.

Buckley, Helen E. *Grandfather and I*. Ill. Jan Ormerod. New York: Lothrop, Lee & Shepard, 1994.

A young boy and his grandfather enjoy spending time together while others hurry along. A rhythmical text featuring an African-American family.

———. *Grandmother and I*. Ill. Jan Ormerod. New York: Lothrop, Lee & Shepard, 1994.

A young girl loves Grandmother's lap best. A warm African-American family story.

Bucknell, Caroline. *One Bear All Alone*. New York: Dial, 1989.

A rhyming counting book featuring anthropomorphic bears.

Bunting, Eve. *Flower Garden*. Ill. Kathryn Hewitt. San Diego, Calif.: Harcourt Brace, 1994.

A young girl prepares a window sill garden for her mother's birthday with the help of her father. A non-European American family.

Burningham, John. *The Blanket*. New York: Crowell, 1976.

A young boy and his blanket with simple text and pictures.

———. *The Dog*. 2nd ed. London: Candlewick Press, 1994.

A young boy who baby-sits a dog and then wants to keep him.

———. *Mr. Gumpy's Motor Car*. New York: Crowell, 1971.

Mr. Gumpy and all his friends, children, and animals alike, go for a ride in his car with surprising results.

———. *Mr. Gumpy's Outing*. New York: H. Holt, 1971.

Everyone invites themselves to go with Mr. Gumpy in his boat, but then things get out of hand.

Butterworth, Nicki. *Jasper's Beanstalk*. New York: Bradbury, 1993.

Jasper the cat plants a beanstalk that does not grow as fast as expected.

Campbell, Rod. *Dear Zoo*. New York: Macmillan, 1983.

A young boy writes to the zoo for a pet with amazing results. A pop-up book that is a real winner.

Carle, Eric. *One, Two, Three to the Zoo*. New York: Putnam, 1989.

A counting, color, and animal book about a train taking animals to the zoo.

———. *The Very Busy Spider*. New York: Philomel, 1994.

A spider does not stop for anything until she finishes her web.

———. *The Very Hungry Caterpillar*. New York: Putnam, 1981.

A popular story of a caterpillar who eats its way through the days of the week and emerges as a butterfly.

Carlson, Nancy. *I Like Me.* New York: Viking, 1990.

An adorable pig child tells how she likes herself and the good things she does for her self-respect.

Carroll, Kathleen Sullivan. *One Red Rooster.* Ill. Suzette Barbier. Boston: Houghton Mifflin, 1992.

A number and counting book of noisy farm animals with a rhyming text.

Cauley, Lorinda. *Three Little Kittens.* New York: Grossett and Dunlap, 1982.

An illustrated version of this famous song.

Charles, N. N. *What Am I? Looking through Shapes at Apples and Grapes.* Ill. Leo and Diane Dillon. New York: Blue Sky Press, 1994.

Color and shape concepts come together in this simple yet complex guessing game book. Ask toddlers what colors lie behind the cutouts, which reveal beautiful fruit. The last two pages reveal a rainbow and then a display of different-colored children's hands.

Child, Lydia Maria. *Over the River and through the Wood.* Ill. Christopher Manson. New York: North-South, 1993.

The Thanksgiving song with uncluttered traditional illustrations.

———. *Over the River and through the Wood.* Ill. Nadine Westcott. New York: HarperCollins, 1993.

The Thanksgiving song with Westcott's more modern illustrations.

Crews, Donald. *Freight Train.* New York: Greenwillow, 1978.

A train's engine and cars and their colors are presented in bold clear illustrations and a very simple text.

———. *Harbor.*

All kinds of boats are presented.

———. *Parade.*

A parade is seen from start to finish.

———. *School Bus.*

The day in the life of yellow school buses.

Dabcovich, Lydia. *Sleepy Bear.* New York: Dutton, 1982.

Fall comes and a bear hibernates and wakes up in spring. The large simple illustrations and text make this a perfect book for programs.

Degan, Bruce. *Jamberry.* New York: HarperCollins, 1983.

A boy and a bear revel in all different kinds of berries. With a clever rhyming text.

DePaola, Tomi. *Baby's First Christmas.* New York: Putnam, 1988. (BB)

One of a series of holiday board books which introduces some of the symbols with colorful illustrations.

———. *My First Chanukah.* New York: Putnam, 1989. (BB)

———. *My First Easter.* New York: Putnam, 1991. (BB)

———. *My First Halloween.* New York: Putnam, 1991. (BB)

———. *My First Passover.* New York: Putnam, 1991. (BB)

———. *My First Thanksgiving.* New York: Putnam, 1992. (BB)

Desimimi, Lisa. *My House.* New York: Henry Holt, 1994.

Describes a house in different seasons, weather, and light conditions with innovative illustrations.

Domanska, Janina. *Busy Monday Morning.* New York: Greenwillow, 1985.

A boy and his father work every day of the week until they rest on Sunday.

Ehlert, Lois. *Feathers for Lunch.* New York: Harcourt Brace, 1990.

Beautiful illustrations and a brief rhyming text show a cat stalking birds with no success.

———. *Growing Vegetable Soup.* New York: Harcourt Brace, 1987.

Beautifully illustrated story of planting a garden and making soup from the results.

———. *Planting a Rainbow.* New York: Harcourt Brace, 1988.

Seeds and plants are planted in the spring and a variety of flowers bloom in beautiful colors.

Falwell, Cathryn. *Feast for Ten.* New York: Clarion, 1993.

This counting book shows an African-American family shopping and preparing a meal together. A rhyming text.

———. *We Have a Baby.* New York: Clarion, 1993.

A baby enters the lives of a family with a young child. The illustrations are ethnically ambiguous, and the gender of the older child is not specified.

Field, Rachel. *General Store.* Ill. Nancy Parker. New York: Greenwillow, 1988.

    A simple story of a general store.

Fleming, Denise. *Barnyard Banter.* New York: Henry Holt, 1994.

    An introduction to different farm animal sounds with lively illustrations.

————. *Counting.* New York: Henry Holt, 1992.

    Color counting book of animals.

————. *In the Small Small Pond.* New York: Henry Holt, 1993.

    Beautiful illustrations and a brief rhyming text explore pond life throughout the year.

————. *In the Tall Tall Grass.* New York: Henry Holt, 1991.

    A toddler's view of many animals found in the grass. A rhyming text with beautiful illustrations.

Florian, Douglas. *An Auto Mechanic.* New York: Greenwillow, 1991.

    The daily work of a mechanic is demonstrated with simple illustrations and text.

————. *At the Zoo.* New York: Crowell, 1992.

    A day at the zoo.

————. *A Beach Day.* New York: Greenwillow, 1990.

    A day at the beach.

————. *A Summer Day.* New York: Greenwillow, 1988.

    Activities are shown that are enjoyed in summer.

————. *A Turtle Day.* New York: Crowell, 1989.

    A day in the life of a turtle.

————. *A Winter Day.* New York: Greenwillow, 1987.

    Activities are shown that are enjoyed in winter.

————. *A Year in the Country.* New York: Greenwillow, 1989.

    Activities are shown during the four seasons.

Fox, Mem. *Hattie and the Fox.* New York: Bradbury, 1988.

    The animals ignore Hattie the Hen's warnings about a threatening fox until it is almost too late. A cumulative text.

Ginsburg, Mirra. *Across the Stream.* Ill. Nancy Tafuri. New York: Greenwillow, 1982.

    Some ducks help a hen and her chicks escape a fox in this story with an elegant rhyming text and lovely illustrations.

————. *Chick and the Duckling.* Ill. Aruego and Ariane Dewey. New York: Macmillan, 1988.

    A chick copies everything a duck does until it comes to swimming.

————. *Good Morning, Chick.* Ill. Byron Barton. New York: Greenwillow, 1980.

    A young chick's day on a farm.

Goennel, Heidi. *Colors.* Boston: Little, Brown, 1990.

    A little girl finds very different things to be the same color.

Gomi, Taro. *Everyone Poops.* Brooklyn, New York: Miller Books, 1993.

    A straightforward look at "pooping" from animals to people in a light humorous style.

Goodspeed, Peter. *A Rhinoceros Wakes Me Up in the Morning.* Ill. Dennis Panek. New York: Puffin, 1984.

    A child imagines his stuffed animals accompanying him throughout the day. A lovely rhyming text.

Greenfield, Eloise. *I Make Music.* Ill. Jan Gilchrist. New York: Writers and Readers, 1991. (BB)

    A young African-American girl is encouraged by her family when she makes music.

————. *My Daddy and I.* Ill. Jan Gilchrist. New York: Writers and Readers, 1991. (BB)

    An African-American boy and his father do chores around the house together.

————. *My Doll, Keshia.* Ill. Jan Gilchrist. New York: Writers and Readers, 1991. (BB)

    A young girl in an African-American family tells about her doll.

Gretz, Susanna. *Teddy Bears 1 to 10.* New York: Macmillan, 1986.

    A rhyming counting book of teddy bear people.

Hale, Sarah. *Mary Had a Little Lamb.* Ill. Tomie DePaola. New York: Holiday, 1984.

    A picture story version of the familiar song.

————. *Mary Had a Little Lamb.* Photographs by Bruce McMillan. New York: Scholastic, 1990.

    A contemporary version of this famous song with lovely photographs of an African-American girl and her lamb.

Hall, Zoe. *It's Pumpkin Time.* Ill. Shari Halpern. New York: Blue Sky Press, 1994.

    Two children plant and watch pumpkins grow, then make Jack-o-Lanterns and go trick-or-treating.

Halpern, Shari. *Little Robin Redbreast: A Mother Goose Rhyme.* New York: North-South, 1994.

This updated version of a cat chasing a bird is brought to life with bright collage pictures.

Harper, Isabelle, and Barry Moser. *My Dog Rosie.* New York: Scholastic, 1994.

A charming story of a young girl who takes care of the family dog while grandfather works in his studio.

Hawkins, Colin, and Jacqui Hawkins. *Old Mother Hubbard.* New York: Putnam, 1985.

A flap book with humorous illustrations from this old rhyme.

Hayes, Sarah. *Eat Up, Gemma.* Ill. Jan Ormerod. New York: Lothrop, 1988.

Baby Gemma refuses to eat until her brother helps out.

Helen, Nancy. *The Bus Stop.* New York: Orchard, 1988.

Different people wait for the bus in this cumulative story, which features partial and cut-out pages.

Hill, Eric. *Spot Bakes a Cake.* New York: Putnam, 1994.

Spot, with a little help from his Mom, makes a birthday cake for his Dad.

———. *Spot Goes to School.* New York: Putnam, 1984.

Spot has an enjoyable first day at school.

———. *Spot Goes to the Circus.* New York: Putnam, 1986.

Spot ends up behind the scenes of a circus looking for his ball.

———. *Spot Goes to the Farm.* New York: Putnam, 1987.

Spot looks for new baby animals on a farm.

———. *Spot's Baby Sister.* New York: Putnam, 1989.

Spot enjoys his new baby sister.

———. *Spot's Birthday Party.* New York: Putnam, 1982.

Spot and his friends play hide and seek at his birthday party.

———. *Spot's First Christmas.* New York: Putnam, 1993.

Spot enjoys the delights of his first Christmas.

———. *Spot's First Easter.* New York: Putnam, 1988.

Spot enjoys his first Easter.

———. *Where's Spot?* New York: Putnam, 1980.

The first "Spot" book, in which we meet a lovable puppy who plays hide and seek with all his animal friends until Mom finds him in time for dinner. A sturdy lift-the-flap series that is always a hit.

Holzenthaler, Jean. *My Hands Can.* Ill. Nancy Tafuri. New York: Dutton, 1978.

The hands of a young child are show doing many things like clapping, zipping, etc. Hands can also hurt and soothe. The simple illustrations are very close up and engaging.

Hudson, Cheryl. *Good Morning Baby.* Ill. George Ford. New York: Scholastic, 1992. (BB)

African-American babies and toddlers enjoy everyday things and activities. A rhyming text.

———. *Good Night Baby.* Ill. George Ford. New York: Scholastic, 1992. (BB)

African-American babies and toddlers get ready for bed. A rhyming text.

Hutchins, Pat. *Happy Birthday, Sam.* New York: Greenwillow, 1978.

On Sam's birthday he is still too short to do many things, but he gets some help from Grandpa's present.

———. *Good-Night, Owl.* New York: Macmillan, 1972.

Owl cannot sleep because a variety of animals are so noisy, they keep him awake. He gets his revenge. This is recommended for use as a felt-board story because the animals in the tree are difficult to see from a distance.

———. *Rosie's Walk.* New York: Macmillan, 1968.

Rosie the hen goes for a walk, oblivious to the fact she is being stalked by a fox. The very brief text introduces the concepts of over, under, through, etc.

Isadora, Rachel. *I Hear.* New York: Greenwillow, 1985.

One of three books, this introduces the concept of sound in a young toddler's world. Lovely soft illustrations and a brief text.

———. *I See.* New York: Greenwillow, 1985.

Introduces the concept of seeing.

———. *I Touch.* New York: Greenwillow, 1985.

Introduces the concept of touch.

Janovitz, Marilyn. *Look out, Bird!* New York: North-South, 1994.

Snail slips off a flower and hits bird on the head, setting off a chain of events that ends back with snail.

Jonas, Ann. *Now We Can Go*. New York: Greenwillow, 1986.

A young child must pack favorite toys before leaving the house.

———. *Two Bear Cubs*. New York: Greenwillow, 1982.

Two bear cubs get lost and found with bright illustrations and a simple text.

———. *When You Were a Baby*. New York: Greenwillow, 1982.

Shows many things a toddler can do that an infant could not.

Joosse, Barbara. *Mama, Do You Love Me?* San Francisco: Chronicle Books, 1991.

Arctic mother reassures her child of her unconditional love for him.

Jorgensen, Gail. *Crocodile Beat*. Ill. Patricia Mullins. New York: Macmillan, 1989.

A lion saves his jungle friends from a crocodile. A rhyming text and animal sounds make this a fun read-aloud.

Kemp, Moira. *Baa, Baa, Black Sheep*. New York: Lodestar, 1991. (BB)

One of four slightly larger board books of well-known nursery rhymes.

———. *Hey Diddle Diddle*. New York: Lodestar, 1991. (BB)

———. *Hickory, Dickory, Dock*. New York: Lodestar, 1991. (BB)

———. *This Little Pig*. New York: Lodestar, 1991. (BB)

Koch, Michelle. *By the Sea*. New York: Greenwillow, 1991.

The concept of opposites is shown by the seashore.

Kraus, Robert. *Where Are You Going, Little Mouse?* Ill. Jose Aruego and Ariane Dewey. New York: Greenwillow, 1986.

A mouse runs away from home only to find that he misses his family. A rhyming text and large colorful illustrations.

———. *Whose Mouse Are You?* Macmillan, 1970.

A lonely mouse child discovers he is not alone because of his family, including a new baby brother.

Kraus, Ruth. *Carrot Seed*. New York: HarperCollins, 1945.

A boy plants and tends a carrot seed while his family tells him it will never grow. Do they get a surprise! A classic.

Lear, Edward. *The Owl and the Pussycat*. Ill. Jan Brett. New York: Putnam, 1991.

A beautifully illustrated version of this poem of an owl and a cat in love.

Lember, Barbara Hirsh. *A Book of Fruit*. New York: Ticknor & Fields, 1994.

Beautiful photographs introduce a variety of fruits and how they grow, on a tree or vine.

Lewin, Hugh. *Jafta*. Ill. Lisa Kopper. New York: Lerner, 1989.

A young African boy pretends he is different animals.

McMillan, Bruce. *Kitten Can*. New York: Lothrop, 1984.

Beautiful photographs show things a kitten can do.

McPhail, David. *Pig Pig Rides*. New York: Dutton, 1982.

Pig Pig has a wonderful day pretending to ride a train to China, jump elephants with a motorcycle, etc.

Maris, Ron. *Are You There, Bear?* New York: Greenwillow, 1985.

A search for Bear in a darkened bedroom.

Marshall, Edward. *Space Case*. Ill. James Marshall. New York: Dial, 1980.

A visitor from space arrives just in time for Halloween. The book is long and should be shortened by not reading it all or shortening the text.

Martin, Bill. *Brown Bear, Brown Bear, What Do You See?* Ill. Eric Carle. New York: Henry Holt, 1992.

A great participation book of color and animal identification. The large illustrations are a plus.

Martin, Bill, and John Archambault. *Chicka Chicka Boom Boom*. Ill. Lois Ehlert. New York: Simon & Schuster, 1989.

A rhyming alphabet book with bright letters dashing up a coconut tree. A wonderful read-aloud with a beat.

———. *Here Are My Hands*. Ill. Ted Rand. New York: Henry Holt, 1989.

A wonderful introduction to parts of the human body with close-up, bright illustrations of multiracial children.

Miller, Margaret. *Whose Hat?* New York: Greenwillow, 1988.

Photographs of different hats that make a great guessing game.

———. *Whose Shoe?* New York: Greenwillow, 1991.

Photographs of different shoes showing different kinds of occupations. It makes a great guessing game.

Morris, Ann. *Bread, Bread, Bread.* Photographs by Ken Heyman. New York: Lothrop, Lee & Shepard, 1989.

Celebrates the many different kinds of bread and how bread is enjoyed all over the world.

———. *Hats, Hats, Hats.* Photographs by Ken Heyman. New York: Lothrop, Lee & Shepard, 1989.

Shows a variety of people and their hats from around the world.

———. *Houses and Homes.* Photographs by Ken Heyman. New York: Lothrop, Lee & Shepard, 1992.

Shows different kinds of dwellings from around the world and the people who live in them.

Noll, Sally. *Off and Counting.* New York: Puffin, 1985.

A wind-up frog in a toy store hops by different numbers of toys.

Norworth, Jack. *Take Me Out to the Ballgame.* New York: Four Winds Press, 1993.

The text is the famous baseball song and the illustrations show the 1949 world series between the Dodgers and the Yankees at Ebbetts Field.

Offen, Hilda. *A Fox Got My Socks.* New York: Dutton, 1992.

The wind blows a toddler's clothes off the clothesline and different animals claim their prize. A rhyming text with finger-game instructions.

Ormerod, Jan. *To Baby with Love.* New York: Lothrop, Lee & Shepard, 1994.

A collection of five simple stories that can be used separately. Includes the familiar finger game, "There Was a Little Turtle."

Oxenbury, Helen. *All Fall Down.* New York: Aladdin, 1987. (BB)

Four cavorting multiracial babies. Perfect for use as a second book in any program.

———. *Clap Hands.* New York: Aladdin, 1987. (BB)

Four cavorting multiracial babies. Perfect for use as a second book in any prgram.

———. *Dressing.* New York: Simon & Schuster, 1981. (BB)

Shows a young child getting dressed.

———. *Family.* New York: Simon & Schuster, 1981. (BB)

Members of a family are introduced, ending with "baby."

———. *Say Good-Night.* New York: Aladdin, 1987. (BB)

Four cavorting multiracial babies. Perfect for use as a second book in any program.

———. *Tickle, Tickle.* New York: Aladdin, 1987. (BB)

Four cavorting multiracial babies. Perfect for use as a second book in any program.

———. *Tom and Pippo and the Dog.* New York: Aladdin, 1989.

While out for a walk, Tom and Pippo have an adventure with a dog.

———. *Tom and Pippo on the Beach.* Cambridge, Mass.: Candlewick Press, 1993.

Tom and Pippo spend the day at the beach.

Paterson, Diane. *Smile for Auntie.* New York: Dial, 1977.

Only when a pushy Aunt leaves does baby smile.

———. *Soap and Suds.* New York: Knopf, 1984.

A woman hangs her laundry out to dry but it does not stay clean long.

Pocock, Rita. *Annabelle and the Big Slide.* New York: Harcourt Brace, 1989.

A little girl finally goes down the big slide in the park all by herself.

Raffi. *Five Little Ducks.* Ill. Jose and Ariane Dewey. New York: Crown, 1988.

When her ducklings disappear one by one, Mother Duck sets out to find them.

Raschka, Chris. *Yo! Yes?* New York: Orchard, 1993.

Two lonely boys, one African American and one white, meet on the street and become friends. The brief snappy text moves along.

Rice, Eve. *Benny Bakes a Cake.* New York: Greenwillow, 1981.

When Benny's birthday cake is eaten by the dog, Papa comes to the rescue.

————. *Goodnight, Goodnight.* New York: Greenwillow, 1980.

Night comes to everyone in town including the cat.

————. *Sam Who Never Forgets.* New York: Greenwillow, 1977.

Sam the Zookeeper never forgets to feed the animals.

Rockwell, Anne. *Boats.* New York: Dutton, 1985.

Shows boats and ships of many sizes and uses.

————. *Cars.* New York: Dutton, 1984.

Shows different cars and their uses.

————. *In Our House.* New York: Crowell, 1985.

Relates activities that take place in different rooms of a house.

Rockwell, Anne and Harlow Rockwell. *How My Garden Grew.* New York: Macmillan, 1982.

A little girl describes growing a garden.

Rockwell, Harlow. *My Nursery School.* New York:

A child describes the various activities found in a nursery school.

Roffey, Maureen and Bernard Lodge. *The Grand Old Duke of York.* New York: Whispering Coyote Press, 1993.

The Duke loses and then finds his men in this old nursery rhyme with new verses.

Scott, Ann Herbert. *On Mother's Lap.* New York: McGraw-Hill, 1972.

A small Eskimo boy discovers that Mother's lap has room for everyone.

Shaw, Nancy. *Sheep in a Jeep.* Ill. Margot Apple. New York: Houghton Mifflin, 1986.

Sheep meet with misadventure when they go for a ride in a jeep. A humorous rhyming text.

————. *Sheep on a Ship.* Ill. Margot Apple. New York: Houghton Mifflin, 1989.

Sheep on a ship run into trouble when a storm blows up.

————. *Sheep Out to Eat.* Ill. Margot Apple. New York: Houghton Mifflin, 1992.

Hungry sheep run into trouble in a tea shop.

————. *Sheep Take a Hike.* Ill. Margot Apple. Boston: Houghton Mifflin, 1994.

Sheep explore the great outdoors only to get lost. They find their way home by following the trail of wool they left.

Siebert, Diane. *Train Song.* Ill. Mike Wimmeer. New York: HarperTrophy, 1993.

A rhyming text makes these different train trips enjoyable.

Slobodkinia, Esphyr. *The Wonderful Feast.* New York: Greenwillow, 1993.

In this reprint of the 1955 classic, Farmer Jones feeds his horse, and what is left is a wonderful feast for many other animals.

Steptoe, John. *Baby Says.* New York: Lothrop, 1988.

A baby and a big brother figure out how to get along.

Tafuri, Nancy. *Have You Seen My Duckling?* New York: Greenwillow, 1984.

A mother duck searches for one of her missing ducklings.

————. *Rabbit's Morning.* New York: Greenwillow, 1985.

A rabbit explores the meadow and sees a variety of other animals.

————. *Spots, Feathers and Curly Tails.* New York: Greenwillow, 1988.

Farm animals are identified in this question and answer book.

————. *This Is the Farmer.* New York: Greenwillow, 1994.

A farmer starts a series of events involving various farm animals by kissing his wife good morning.

Titherington, Jeanne. *Baby's Boat.* New York: Greenwillow, 1992.

A beautifully illustrated poem describing a baby sailing out in a silver moon boat.

————. *Pumpkin, Pumpkin.* New York: Greenwillow, 1986.

A boy plants pumpkin seeds, watches them grow, and carves a jack-o-lantern for Halloween.

Wallwork, Amanda. *No Dodos: A Counting Book of Endangered Animals.* New York: Scholastic, 1993.

A bright and simple counting book of animals from whales to pandas.

Walsh, Ellen. *Hop Jump.* San Diego: Harcourt Brace, 1993.

Bored with hopping and jumping, a frog discovers dancing.

Watanabe, Shigeo. *How Do I Put It On?* Ill. Yasuo Ohtomo. New York: Philomel, 1984.

A bear child demonstrates the wrong and right way to put on clothes.

————. *What a Good Lunch.* New York: Philomel, 1991.

A bear child overcomes difficulties and manages to eat lunch all by himself.

———. *Where's My Daddy?* New York: Philomel, 1991.

A bear child searches for his Daddy.

Weiss, Nicki. *Sun, Sand, Sea, Sail.* New York: Greenwillow, 1989.

A family picnics by the sea and enjoys many activities.

———. *Where Does the Brown Bear Go?* New York: Greenwillow, 1989.

A variety of animals go home to bed.

Wells, Rosemary. *Max's Birthday.* New York: Dial, 1985. (BB)

Sister Ruby gives Max a wind-up toy dragon for his birthday.

———. *Max's Breakfast.* New York: Dial, 1985. (BB)

Max's sister tries hard to get him to eat his egg.

———. *Max's Chocolate Chicken.* New York: Dial, 1989.

Max and Ruby go on an Easter egg hunt, each wanting the prize chocolate chicken.

———. *Max's Christmas.* New York: Dial, 1986.

Max waits up for Santa on Christmas Eve.

———. *Max's First Word.* New York: Dial, 1979. (BB)

Sister Ruby encourages Max to say all kinds of simple words, but he comes up with "delicious."

Williams, Sue. *I Went Walking.* San Diego: Harcourt Brace, 1990.

A growing parade of farm animals follows a toddler on a walk. Rhythmic text.

Williams, Vera. *"More, More, More," Said the Baby.*

Three babies given love and kisses by a father, grandmother, and mother.

Wishsky, Frieda. *Oonga Boonga.* Ill. Sucie Stevenson. Boston: Little Brown, 1990.

A crying baby is soothed by brother's nonsense phrases.

Wolff, Ashley. *A Year of Beasts.* New York: Dutton, 1986.

Two children see many animals around their country house throughout the year.

———. *A Year of Birds.* New York: Dodd, Mead, 1984.

Many kinds of birds visit a child's home during each month of the year.

Yolen, Jane. *Mouse's Birthday.* Ill. Bruce Degan. New York: Putnam, 1993.

A mouse's haystack home is overcrowded when his friends come to celebrate his birthday. A rhyming text.

Youngs, Betty. *Pink Pigs in Mud: A Color Book.* New York: Merrimack, 1985.

Farm animals of different colors are introduced.

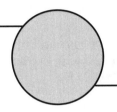

Further Reading and Resources

Best Loved Songs and Hymns. Ed. James Morehead. Cleveland: World, 1965.

This includes hard-to-find spirituals and other songs.

Brown, Marc. *Finger Rhymes*. New York: Dutton, 1980.

A collection of fourteen well-known finger games with instructions and nice black-and-white illustrations.

Butler, Dorothy. *Babies Need Books*. New York: Atheneum, 1982.

A mandate to make books a part of every baby's life from birth on. Highly recommended.

Chinese Mother Goose Rhymes. Ed. Robert Wyndham. Ill. Ed Young. New York: Philomel, 1989, 1968.

A collection of nursery rhymes translated from Chinese. Also includes the rhymes in Chinese characters.

Chorao, Kay. *Mother Goose Magic*. New York: Dutton, 1994.

Eight not-so-familiar nursery rhymes. As each rhyme ends, the characters continue into the next and end up snuggling together in bed.

De Angeli, Marguerite. *Book of Nursery and Mother Goose Rhymes*. Garden City, N.Y.: Doubleday, 1954.

A large collection of 376 of the more usual rhymes.

"De Colores" and Other Latin-American Folk Songs for Children. Selected, arranged, and translated by Jose Luis Orozco. New York: Dutton, 1994.

A bilingual collection of songs for special times from Spanish-speaking countries.

Defty, Jeff. *Creative Fingerplays and Action Rhymes: An Index and Guide to Their Uses*. Phoenix: Oryx Press, 1992.

A reference guide for locating finger games.

Finger Frolics. Comp. Liz Cromwell, et al. Ill. Joan Lockwood. Mt. Rainier, Md.: Gryphon, 1983.

A collection of many finger games with instructions, organized by subject.

Fireside Book of Fun and Game Songs. Ed. Marie Winn with musical arrangements by Allan Miller. Ill. Whitney Darrow, Jr. New York: Simon & Schuster, 1974.

A large collection of fun songs in categories from cumulative and easy refrain songs to motion songs. All have musical arrangements, guitar chords, and directions.

Fireside Song Book of Birds and Beasts. Comp. and ed. Jane Yolen. New York: Simon & Schuster, 1972.

A large collection that contains such favorites as "Where, Oh Where Has My Little Dog Gone?" and "Be Kind to Your Webfooted Friends." Music, guitar chords, and a little history of each song are included.

First Steps to Literacy: Library Programs for Parents, Teachers, and Caregivers. Prepared by the Preschool Services and Parent Education Committee, Association for Library Services to Children. Chicago: American Library Association, 1990.

A potpourri of programs and thoughts about children and library programs. Thought provoking and highly recommended.

Fisher, Aileen. *Feathered Ones and Furry.* Ill. Eric Carle. New York: Crowell, 1971.

Brief poems on animals and nature, many of which can be used as lap jogs, finger games, etc.

Glass, Paul. *Songs and Stories of Afro-Americans.* Ill. Richard Cuffari. New York: Grosset & Dunlap, 1971.

Songs from the African-American tradition from spirituals to the civil rights movement. There are many lengthy historical notes along with musical arrangements and guitar chords.

Glazer, Tom. *Do Your Ears Hang Low? Fifty More Musical Fingerplays.* Ill. Mila Lazarevich. New York: Doubleday, 1980.

A variety of songs, some with new lyrics, with finger-game instructions and musical arrangements with guitar chords.

———. *Eye Winker, Tom Tinker, Chin Chopper: Fifty Musical Fingerplays.* Ill. Ron Himler. Garden City, N.Y.: Doubleday, 1973.

A collection of well-known songs and finger games with instructions, musical arrangements, and guitar chords.

———. *Music for Ones and Twos: Songs and Games for the Very Young.* Garden City, N.Y.: Doubleday, 1983.

A collection of songs and finger games with music and guitar chords.

Go In and Out the Window: An Illustrated Songbook for Young People. Music arranged and edited by Dan Fox. Commentary by Claude Marks. New York: The Metropolitan Museum of Art. Henry Holt, 1987.

An unusual collection of children's favorites; each is presented with a work of art, a historical note, and musical arrangements with guitar chords.

Gonna Sing My Head Off! Collected and arranged by Kathleen Krull. New York: Knopf, 1992.

A great collection of American folk songs from the traditional "Oh, Susanna" to the modern "What Have They Done to the Rain" by Malvina Reynolds.

Greene, Ellin. *Books, Babies and Libraries: Serving Infants, Toddlers, Their Parents and Caregivers.* Chicago: American Library Association, 1991.

An excellent introduction of ideas and the variety of library services for young children and their caregivers.

I'm Going to Sing: Black American Spirituals, Volume 2. Selected and illustrated by Ashley Bryan. New York: Atheneum, 1984.

Some of the best-loved spirituals are included in this second volume with beautiful Bryan illustrations. *Walk Together Children* is the first volume.

Lavender's Blue: A Book of Nursery Rhymes. Comp. Kathleen Lines. Ill. Harold Jones. New York: Franklin Watts, 1954.

An older but lovely collection of nursery rhymes with color and black-and-white illustrations.

Lift Every Voice and Sing: A Collection of Afro-American Spirituals and Other Songs. New York: Church Hymnal Corporation, 1981.

This includes hard-to-find spirituals like "This Little Light of Mine".

Lullaby Songbook. Ed. Jane Yolen with musical arrangements by Adam Stemple. Ill. Charles Mikolaycak. San Diego: Harcourt Brace, 1986.

A collection of fifteen lullabies, each with a historic note and a musical arrangement including guitar chords. The illustrations are lovely.

Mahoney, Ellen, and Leah Wilcox. *Ready, Set, Read: Best Books to Prepare Preschoolers.* Metuchen, N.J.: Scarecrow Press, 1985.

This wonderful resource covers language acquisition and explains why literature is so important for children birth to age five.

Make a Joyful Sound. Poems for Children by African-American Poets. Ed. Deborah Slier. Ill. Cornelius Van Wright and Ying-Hwa Hu. New York: Checkerboard Press, 1991.

A few of the selections are short enough and have lots of rhythm to be perfect for programs. They eloquently speak of childhood and the African-American experience.

Merriam, Eve. *You Be Good and I'll Be Night: Jump-on-the-Bed Poems.* Ill. Karen Lee Schmidt. New York: Morrow, 1988.

A terrific collection of original poems and lovely illustrations.

Ormerod, Jan. *Rhymes around the Day.* Chosen by Pat Thomson. New York: Lothrop, Lee & Shepard, 1983.

Mostly well-known rhymes, in a picture book format with color illustrations by Ormerod, following children's activities from morning until bedtime.

Pomerantz, Charlotte. *Tamarindo Puppy.* Ill. Bryan Barton. New York: Greenwillow, 1980.

A collection of poems with Spanish sprinkled in. Aimed at older children, but a few poems work well with babies and toddlers.

Poston, Elizabeth. *The Baby's Songbook.* Ill. William Stobbs. New York: Crowell, 1971.

A collection of older songs, some of them Mother Goose rhymes, with musical arrangements.

Raffi. *The Raffi Singable Songbook.* New York: Crown, 1980.

Fifty-one songs from Raffi's first three recordings which include many popular songs for today's children. Music and guitar chords included.

Reader's Digest Children's Songbook. Pleasantville, N.Y.: Reader's Digest Assoc., 1985.

A wonderful collection of modern and traditional favorites. Includes songs from movies and shows, cartoons such as "The Teddy Bears' Picnic," "Peter Cottontail," and "Over the Rainbow." Contains musical arrangements and guitar chords. Highly recommended for those hard-to-find popular songs.

The Real Mother Goose. Ill. Blanche Fisher Wright. New York: Checkerboard Press, 1916, 1944.

A very large and very good collection of Mother Goose rhymes with the original 1916 edition illustrations.

Ring a Ring o' Roses: Stories, Games and Finger Plays for Pre-School Children. Flint, Michigan: Flint Public Library, 1971.

An extensive collection of finger games with directions and subject access. Highly recommended.

Ring-a-Ring o' Roses and a Ding, Dong, Bell. Selected and ill. by Allan Marks. Saxonville, Mass.: Picture Book Studio, 1991.

A collection of traditional nursery rhymes with beautiful illustrations.

Ring-a-Round: A Collection of Verse for Boys and Girls. Comp. Mildred Harrington. Ill. Corydon Bell. New York: Macmillan, 1930.

Poems by many famous poets, arranged by subject. The shorter poems lends themselves well to lap jogs, finger games, etc.

Sierra, Judy. *Mother Goose's Playhouse: Toddler Tales and Nursery Rhymes with Patterns for Puppets and Feltboard.* Published by Bob Kaminski Media Arts, 183 Garfield St., Ashland, OR 97520. 505-482-1328.

A good source of craft ideas for baby-toddler programs.

Singing Bee! A Collection of Favorite Children's Songs. Comp. Jane Hart. Ill. Anita Lobel. New York: Lothrop, Lee & Shepard, 1982.

A lovely collection with color illustrations, short historic notes, a subject index and musical arrangements including guitar chords and chord diagrams.

Snow, Barbara. *Index of Songs on Children's Recordings.* 2nd ed. Eugene, Ore.: Staccato Press, 1993.

A good reference tool for locating recorded songs.

Songs America Sings: 121 All-Time Sing-Along Hits in Easy-to-Play Arrangements for Piano, Voice, and Guitar. Comp. Melvin Stecher, Norman Horowitz, and Claire Gordon. New York: G. Schirmer, 1982.

A large collection of standard songs including "America the Beautiful," "Waltzing Matilda," and "When the Saints Go Marching In." Each has a brief historical note.

Songs of Peace, Freedom and Protest. Collected and edited by Tom Glazer. New York: McKay, 1970.

Includes such songs as "This Little Light of Mine" and other favorites.

Songs That Children Sing. Comp. and ed. Eleanor Chroman. New York: Oak Publications, 1970.

A collection of songs from twenty-nine countries from around the world in twenty-five different languages with English translations. Includes guitar chords and simple piano accompaniment.

This Little Pig Went to Market. Play rhymes compiled by Norah Lofts. Ill. Margaret Gill. New York: Franklin Watts, 1966.

A great collection of nursery rhymes showing how to use them as toe and finger counting, tickles, foot patting, etc., for the youngest child.

Tortillitas Para Mamá and Other Nursery Rhymes: Spanish and English. Selected and translated by Margot C. Griego et al. Ill. Barbara Cooney. New York: Holt, Rinehart & Winston, 1981.

This collection of rhymes is in both English and Spanish. Collected from the Spanish communities in the Americas. Many have instructions to accompany the finger game.

Trot Trot to Boston: Play Rhymes for Baby. Comp. Carol F. Ra. Ill. Catherine Stock. New York: Lothrop, Lee & Shepard, 1987.

A beautiful collection of rhymes with instructions for the youngest child in a picture book format.

Venture into Culture: A Resource Book of Multicultural Materials and Programs. Ed. Carla D. Hayden. Chicago: American Library Association, 1992.

Though the book is aimed at older children, the information on holidays and activities is useful and informative. Many ideas can be adapted for the baby-toddler program.

Walk Together Children: Black American Spirituals, Volume 1. Selected and illustrated by Ashley Bryan. New York: Atheneum, 1974.

A collection of well-known spirituals with beautiful illustrations. A second volume is titled *I'm Going to Sing.*

Watson, Clyde. *Catch Me and Kiss Me and Say It Again.* Ill. Wendy Watson. New York: Philomel, 1978.

Original and delightful rhymes, lullabies, and games for the very young child. Highly recommended.

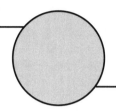

Multilingual and Multicultural Resources

Constructive Playthings, 1227 East 119th St., Grandview, MO 64030-1117. 800-448-4115 or FAX 816-761-9295.

They have a catalog of "Culturally Diverse Materials for Anti-Bias Curriculums" that contains rhythm band instruments, puzzles, recordings, books, etc.

Empak Publishing Company, Dept. C, 212 E. Ohio St., Chicago, IL 60611. 800-477-4554 or FAX 312-642-9657.

They have a "Black History Catalog" that contains many beautiful posters. Most of the other items are very good but are aimed at older children.

Mariuccia Iaconi Book Imports, 970 Tennessee St., San Francisco, CA 94107. 800-955-9577 or 415-826-1216 or FAX 415-821-1596.

Iaconi specializes in Spanish children's literature and has an excellent catalog with indexes for easy use.

Multicultural Distributing Center, 800 Grand Ave., Corvina, CA 91724. 818-859-3133 or FAX 818-859-3136.

A large and wonderful catalog of many language picture stories, some in their original language and some translations. An index is provided for easy access.

National Association for the Education of Young Children, 1509 16th St. N.W., Washington, DC 20036-1426. 800-424-2460 or 202-232-8777 or FAX 202-328-1846.

They have an "Early Childhood Resources Catalog" that has a nice collection of posters. Also of interest are the many titles about early childhood for professionals.

Pan Asian Publications, 29564 Union City Blvd., Union City, CA 94587. 510-475-1185 or FAX 510-475-1489.

A collection of Asian language materials including recordings and bilingual versions of a few picture stories including some "Spot" books by Eric Hill.

Shen's Books and Supplies, 821 S. First Ave., Arcadia, CA 91006. 818-445-6958 or FAX 818-445-6940.

Specializes in the translation of Chinese, Japanese, Korean, and most Southeast Asian languages into English or vice versa. Includes *Rosie's Walk* by Pat Hutchins in Chinese and *The Very Hungry Caterpillar* by Eric Carle in Japanese and Chinese. Highly recommended.

Ventures into Cultures: A Resource Book of Multicultural Materials and Programs. Ed. by Carla D. Hayden. Chicago: American Library Association, 1992.

Lists vendors and publishers of African-American, Arabic, Asian, Hispanic, Jewish, Native American, and Persian materials.

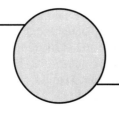

Index

As a youth services librarian with the main children's department of San Francisco Public Library, the late Debby Jeffery developed and presented lapsit programs for infants and toddlers. She later worked in the Office of Children's Services. A graduate of the library school of University of California-Berkeley, Jeffery believed passionately that lapsit children develop into lifelong readers and supporters of libraries.